It Will All Make Sense When You're Dead

Messages from Our
Loved Ones in the Spirit World

PRISCILLA A. KERESEY

LIVE & LEARN
New York

Published By
Live & Learn
P.O. Box 226
Putnam Valley, NY 10579

Orders: www.liveandlearnguides.com

ISBN: 978-0-578-09366-6

Printed in the United States of America

For Jefe

ACKNOWLEDGMENTS

I could never have written this book alone. I owe thanks to my guides and ancestors—my team on the other side—who nagged me until I got their stories down. To all the spirit people who came through in readings, thank you for teaching me how to translate your stories of courage, love, and forgiveness.

Heartfelt thanks to my clients and guests; because of you I have the rare privilege of getting up in the morning and doing work that I love. I'm so grateful that you trust me and this process, and I hope that I have fulfilled the promises I made to you.

To my friends and family, whom I practically ignored during the writing and publishing of this book, thank you for your support, understanding, and patience.

First, last, and always, thanks to God for inspiring me and sustaining me, especially when I feel fear and self-doubt.

We give our loved ones back to God.
And just as He first gave them to us and did not lose them in the giving,
so we have not lost them in returning them to Him.
For life is eternal. Love is immortal. Death is only a horizon
and a horizon is nothing but the limit of our earthly sight.
-Author Unknown

TABLE OF CONTENTS

AUTHOR'S NOTE

The individual experiences recounted in this book are true. However, names and other descriptive details have been changed to protect the identities of people involved. Sentences, phrases, and dialogues in quotes have been taken directly from notes or recordings of actual readings or message circles I've conducted. Most of the dialogues quoted here are verbatim, though some quotes have been edited for clarity only.

Mediumship is the art of translation. When speaking for a spirit person, I may adjust or correct something I've already begun to say. I may repeat myself until I'm satisfied that I have delivered the spirit's message accurately. To illustrate this, I've retained the repetitive or run-on style of dialogue in one or two instances.

Spirit people, mediums, and clients are equally represented by both genders. To that end, I switch pronouns freely throughout this book.

INTRODUCTION

I keep seeing an octopus on the inside surface of my closed eyelids, and it just won't go away. It appears sideways, head on the left and tentacles all stretched to my right, just floating there.

I ignore it and keep talking to my client, who is paying $150 for a private hour with me. Sue, who will become quite a gifted psychic medium herself in the next few years, is sitting eagerly on the edge of her chair across from me. When I open my eyes, I see that *her* eyes are glued to my lips, as if she's willing them to form the words she's been waiting to hear.

We're talking about her minister grandfather, long dead. He's here in the room with us, in my awareness anyway, offering a kind of spiritual support. His wife joins him, followed by Sue's mother. They all show me such specific details of their identity that Sue is satisfied I'm not just making the whole thing up. Despite some sadness and trauma in her youth, Sue and the spirit people are having a pretty happy reunion.

And yet, this octopus.

It hovers here, overlaying the whole transparent group of spirit people. My experience tells me that psychic impressions and spirit communications are defined in part by their persistence. My experience also tells me that ninety percent of all the impressions that come through are symbolic, and it's part of my job as a medium to decode the symbol and translate it to the client.

Let's say a client asks me to shed some light on a career change he's contemplating. In response, I get the impression—through clairvoyance—of a record going around and around on a turntable. Because most of the time the impressions I get are symbolic, I wait for a moment to see what sort of feeling this turntable evokes in me. By concentrating on this turntable, I may soon become aware of the feeling of just going around in circles, of treading the same old ground, and of going nowhere forward. When I feel that my internal interpretation of the symbol is complete, I would say to that client something like, "If you change careers I feel that you won't be addressing the feeling of being on a treadmill. I feel that in a short time you'll be going around the same issues all over again."

If I should concentrate on the turntable in my mind, wait for a feeling, and get nothing, then I assume the turntable is meant to be literal and not symbolic. I may say to the client something like, "I see a venture into music or recording."

For forty-five minutes of my reading with Sue, I've been aware of this octopus and have been waiting for the next part, the feeling it evokes, so I can put it into words for my client. And I get... nothing. No feeling, just octopus.

I continue to ignore it, knowing eventually I will have some sort of feeling about this creature overlaying everything that's coming through. I mean, it *has to be* symbolic, right? I know Sue isn't a marine biologist, or an exotic veterinarian. She's a stay-at-home-mom for heaven's sake. What the heck would a literal octopus be doing in her reading?

I try to force myself to attach a feeling to it. Maybe she's feeling like lots of hands are pulling her in different directions. She has four kids, so that's possible, isn't it? Maybe she's in deep water, over her head. Oh God, maybe she has a brain tumor or something! Yet every time I try to feel one of these interpretations, it seems to slide right off.

Finally, because we're running out of time and I'm nearly breathless with curiosity, I say to Sue, "I don't know what this is, but I'm just going to tell you what I see. Maybe together we can make sense of this."

(My teachers would kill me for breaking a cardinal rule of readings. Never, never, never leave it up to the client to interpret the symbols!).

"I see, oh gosh, I'm sorry. I see, um—jeez, I'm so embarrassed—I see an octopus."

Well, you would have thought I'd just informed Sue she'd won the lottery and would never have to work another day in her life. She shoots up out of her chair, pen and notebook flying, she's shouting, crying, laughing and hugging me all at once. And there I am, feeling awfully proud of myself and acting like I knew this would happen all along. At the same time I'm thinking, "Spit it out lady, what the heck does this mean to you?"

It turns out her former fiancé had passed away before their wedding. His name was Jacobus, and she had lovingly nicknamed him Octopus.

With her validation, a whole flood of new information and messages come through, and another satisfied customer leaves my office. I make a promise to myself that in the future I will not wait, but I will say *exactly* what comes through.

That was years ago, but to this day I still find myself letting rational thought leak into my readings. At a message circle just last week I kept seeing a butterfly over the guest to my left. She and her family were enjoying a visit from her sister in spirit, who had passed from uterine cancer. Every guest had received a unique message, with deeply personal details. It was the kind of wonderful event where it seems everyone, for a moment anyway, truly believes that death isn't real, and that they're really all together again. Maybe they'll doubt their experience later on at home, but for now there is a genuine connection in the present moment.

The butterfly evoked no feeling in me during the circle, so I recognized the need for a literal interpretation. My conscious mind was arguing with me, however: *A butterfly? Come on, is that the best you can do? If you say that you'll sound just like those fake New Age mediums who wax poetic about the eternal nature of love and offer vague, abstract "messages" from who-could-ever-prove-it Native American spirit guides.*

So I said nothing. After the circle was over we were all chatting, and the subject of childhood nicknames came up. Guess what? The guest to my left had been dubbed "Butterfly" by her dead sister. Part of me wanted to leap up and say, "I saw that! She had that all around you!" But no one has faith in a medium who tells you she sees what you already told her.

Once again I vowed to myself and the spirit people, "I promise I will say exactly what you impress on me."

And boy, have they been impressing me to write this book!

What follows is a story of how my mediumship career unfolded. The patience and persistence of my own and my clients' spirit people have been instrumental in my work and in writing this book. While my clients here in the physical world are the ones who pay me to translate between the other dimension and this one, I am equally obliged to the spirit people. I consider them to be my clients on the other side. For the past year or so these spirit people have been nagging at me to sit down and tell these tales. They want me to tell you how they spend their time, and how contacting a spirit person can lighten the burden of grief, guilt, or regret.

They want me to teach you how you, too, can develop the skill of mediumship.

These ancestors, friends, and colleagues want me to tell you that even though physical death has intervened, forgiveness can still be given and received. Most importantly, they want me to show you that love and life continue, that they're still part of the family and witnessing both important events and little moments, and that we will all meet again in good time.

They are always delighted when a physical loved one comes calling, and are eager to share their perspective on their time in the physical world. As more than one spirit has cheerfully told me: *It will all make sense when you're dead!*

Priscilla Keresey
New York, September 27, 2011

GLOSSARY OF TERMS

Not everyone is familiar with psychic mediumship. This short list will explain the terms you'll be seeing throughout this book, though it is not a comprehensive dictionary of all phrases related to this field. Some of these terms were given to me by the spirit people themselves, or are unique to my experience, and may not be found in other authors' usage.

Belong
A spirit person belongs to the guest who recognizes and identifies him. The guest also belongs to the spirit person who comes through.

Bring In or Bring Through
When I become aware of a spirit person, I introduce or bring her through to my client.

Client
A person who come to me for a one-on-one reading.

Cold Reading
A series of techniques used by illusionists to determine details about another person, often in order to convince them that the reader knows much more about a subject than they actually do. Without prior knowledge of a person, a practiced cold reader can still quickly obtain a great deal of information about the subject by analyzing the person's body language, age, gender, race, manner of speech, and so on. Cold readers commonly employ high probability guesses about the subject, picking up on signals from their subjects as to whether their guesses are in the right direction or not, and then reinforcing any chance connections the subjects acknowledge while quickly moving on from missed guesses. (Source: Wikipedia)

Come In
To be born. Spirit people often talk about new spirits who are getting ready to come in.

Go Out
How the spirit people define leaving the physical body at the time of death. I have heard them say, "I went out after a long battle with cancer," or "She came out after I did." We say a person has died; spirit people say they went out to the spirit world.

Guests
People who attend message circles, usually strangers to each other.

Medium
A person who can see, feel, or hear the presence of a spirit person. Most mediums are also psychics. You'll find more information about being a psychic medium in Chapter 2.

Message
What a spirit person asks me to convey to a client or guest.

Message Circle
A more modern term for séance. In a message circle, four to twenty people sit in a circle with the expectation of receiving a message from a loved one who has passed away. I tune into my sixth sense and bring the spirit people through. Once they're identified by a guest, I give their message. A complete description can be found in the *The Setting* section of Chapter 2 and in more detail in Chapter 12.

Physical Mediumship
Manifesting evidence of the spirit into a material object: a voice, moving a table, creating artwork, and so on. It is extremely rare.

Piggy-backing
When spirit people share details in common, and appear together. An example of piggy-backing is in Chapter 2.

Psychic
A person who uses his sixth sense to see, hear, or feel subtle information in the physical world, about the physical world. Many psychics are also mediums.

Reading
Sharing information gathered from the sixth sense or spirit people, generally in a half-hour or one-hour long one-on-one appointment with a client. A psychic medium brings in spirit people and offers insight into the future, relationships, career, and so on.

Spirit Guide
Descriptions of spirit guides differ, depending on the source. In this book I refer to spirit guides as those spirits who didn't live on earth as a human being, and are generally wiser and more forgiving than us mortals. I don't introduce them in readings or circles except when asked, as their presence cannot truly be validated.

Spirit Person or Spirit People
These are the spirits who appear to me during readings or message circles. They are known to my physical clients either as colleagues, schoolmates, friends, loved ones, ancestors, or other family members who have died. We also see spirit animals during readings and circles.

Spirit World
Where the spirit people reside after leaving their human bodies.

Symbols
How information is most effectively conveyed through the sixth sense. More information about symbols is in the *The Language of Spirit People* section of Chapter 2.

Tune in
I use this term to describe how I ignore my five physical senses, and turn all of my concentration and focus to my sixth sense. In doing so, I can see, feel and hear the spirit people and their messages.

PART ONE

The Beginning

CHAPTER 1

Gift or Skill?

I'm asked these kinds of questions on a regular basis:

"When did you know you had... (dramatic pause)... *the gift?*"

"Were you born with a veil?"

"Did you have a near death experience as a child?"

"Were you initiated through some kind of school or guru?"

I wish I could say that something dramatic happened to me, because it might make the story so much more interesting. But the boring fact is that I had a perfectly normal, healthy childhood. Did I have psychic experiences as a child, or see things before they happened, or know before anyone else did that old Uncle Bill was going to die? Sure I did. I believe all children have psychic experiences before we're told to "stop daydreaming." The sixth sense feels perfectly natural to a healthy little person because it's a perfectly natural sense we're all born possessing. It's only through exposure to the world of adults and society that we learn to tune out our own natural psychic abilities, and to rely mostly on what the five physical senses report to us.

If I were interested in creating a rarefied persona that had been somehow specially chosen to communicate with the dead, it would be necessary to back that up with some fantastic occurrence beyond my—and therefore your—control. Something that you, poor reader, weren't lucky enough to experience. If that's the case, you won't ever acquire the kind of gift I'm able to bestow on my fortunate clients.

That fact is, I developed this skill through plain old hard work and practice. At the end of this book I'll show you how you can do it, too. When people ask me how I acquired *the gift* or when I knew I had it, I tell them all the same thing: I don't think mediumship is a gift, I think it's a skill. If there is any gift in what I do, it's in the artful use of that skill—being sensitive and compassionate with my clients. There is an art to listening and communicating sometimes difficult information, but I believe that, too, can be developed with discipline and practice.

Discovering My Abilities

I do remember some non-rational experiences I had as a kid, but I bet you had similar experiences yourself. For example, I can remember, up until the time I was about thirteen years old, being spontaneously and randomly out of my body—and I didn't like it one bit. The clearest memory I have was the last time it happened. I was babysitting and the kids were already asleep. I got up to get a soda from the kitchen, and as I walked back toward the couch my sense of self suddenly seemed to change. It was as if I were behind and slightly above my own right shoulder. It seemed as though my eyesight and thoughts originated from that position, instead of from within my own body. I could actually see my shoulder, my right cheek and my hair as it fell from the top of my head down my back. I seemed to be watching my body walk toward a couch and sit down—feeling not a part of it, but rather attached to it and trailing behind as it moved about the room. At the same time I remember feeling frustration that this was happening again. It felt foreign and bizarre. I was hoping it would be over before the parents came home, because in the past when I'd had to talk to people I would think what I needed to say then listen to this girl say it a fraction of a second later.

That experience had happened to me a handful of times in the past, though I don't remember all the details. I just know it must have happened before because when it happened while I was babysitting, I remember being angry about it happening—again. The process seemed altogether random at the time, and I didn't seem to have any ability to get back into my body. When I tried, I just slid off. I knew from past experience that I just had to wait it out, and this time I remember feeling very strongly that I didn't want it to happen again. It never did.

Once when I was about fourteen I stared at the rosebush outside our door and willed it to move, even though there wasn't a breeze. It did, or I thought it did, and I succeeded in truly freaking myself out.

Right after college, I visited my friend at her home, and, as I was falling asleep on my makeshift bed on the den floor, I heard a little child laughing. I rolled over and had the distinct impression of a little curly-headed toddler giggling away. When I blinked, he was gone.

In my early twenties, I was thinking about a bridge collapsing and cars going into the water. I don't know why I was thinking about it; it had the quality of a daydream. You know that blissful feeling of daydreaming? Your conscious mind knows you have to get back to work but it just feels so relaxing to let a story play out in your imagination. I had a conscious mind thought that ran something like this: "Wow, are you weird or what? Why the heck are you daydreaming about a bridge collapsing?" Yet I kept on with it for a little while. Now, sometimes when I daydream about disasters it's so I can be the hero (come on, admit it, you do it, too). *Is that a car accident up ahead? I'll leap off my still-moving motorcycle and pull someone out of the wreckage!* I wasn't in this daydream however, simply observing it.

The following day at 1:30 a.m. on June 28, 1983, the Mianus River Bridge on I-95 collapsed and three people died when their cars fell with the bridge. As you can imagine, a part of my mind accused me of actually creating this accident! It never occurred to me that it was a premonition.

Various random incidents like this cropped up out throughout my life, though as I matured the frequency diminished. I would still get random hits, such as knowing when someone was pregnant (or the gender of their baby) before they did, or having dreams of such an unusual quality that I knew it was more than my psyche taking out the daily trash. Once during a meditation I clearly remember what it felt like to go out—in other words, what it felt like to die. I had the sense of being hurled into a blackness so complete and infinite that I remember screaming at the top of my lungs and making no sound. The endless vacuum around me was alarming. I felt totally nonphysical, as if I had been a vapor contained in a jar, and the jar disappeared, leaving me to expand uncontrollably in all directions. Within a space of time that felt both instantaneous and eternal I felt separate points of awareness rushing towards me. I recognized them somehow, and knew in a way I can't explain that I was replaying a sudden, accidental death. My welcoming committee on the other side had been unprepared to catch me when I went out.

Another memorable experience stands out from a mountaineering accident I was involved in while climbing the south face of Aconcagua in the Andes. My partner and I were working our way up the sheer south face of rock and ice, and were on our second-to-last day of the ascent. It is an extremely challenging climb in the best of conditions, and we were finishing the day at a very high altitude. I made a stupid mistake and ended up falling almost ninety feet—nearly pulling my partner off the mountain and killing us both. He dug a shallow snow cave where we spent a freezing, uncomfortable night. My ankle was broken and ligaments torn, yet we decided the best course of action was to continue the next day up to the summit. The north side had a descent that was gentler and much more populated, and we'd be able to find assistance and medical care there on the walk down.

The next day I was unable to continue. There was still very difficult climbing ahead, the altitude was slowing down an already slow ascent, and I wasn't sure my ankle would be able to hold out during the final pitches of rock and ice. Once committed on that final part, we would be unable to back off.

Reluctantly, we began a long and dangerous rappel back down the south face. What kept us going was thinking about the stash of food and energy drink we'd left in our small tent near the bottom. At one point, to our great surprise, we met two climbers coming up. As they passed us and heard our story of injury and retreat, they shared their drinks and food with us. We were so grateful for their appearance. Later we watched them climb up and out of sight, critiquing their technique (as climbers often do when watching someone else climb) as incredibly careless and sometimes downright dangerous. A day later when we reached our altitude camp, we found that the climbers who had so generously shared with us were actually sharing our stash! All of the energy powder was gone. The fuel was gone, too, which meant we couldn't melt snow to make water. They'd taken the cookies and strewn the pasta all over the tent. They even took my knife.

Later that night, sleeping huddled together in the tent, a strong feeling woke me. My partner was asleep, so I quietly unzipped the tent flap and hobbled outside into a beautiful, clear, frosty-cold Argentine evening. I was looking at the stars, feeling sorry for myself and our aborted climb, when I felt that strong, nagging feeling again. As I looked up the ridge, I saw the two climbers who'd robbed us and kept our food anyway, even after they'd learned we were in distress. I shook my head and looked again, and they still stood there, high up above me, as though they were made of glass. I knew then that even though their bodies hadn't fallen past us in the night, they were dead.

Honing My Abilities

In my early thirties, while exploring all the wonderful New Age modalities New York City had to offer, I began to notice and enjoy random psychic hits more often. I wondered whether or not I could actually have some control over them. Like many, I'd believed psychic ability was a rare gift bestowed by mysterious forces at an early age, or conveyed solely through the actions of someone wiser or holier than I. Perhaps by some guru, who would open my third eye or turn on my sixth sense after an expensive course of study and an initiation.

I was also a bit intimidated by the notion that inexperienced people like me could stumble upon evil forces or accidentally open a spiritual door, unleashing dark powers that would follow me the rest of my days. The fact was, I really knew nothing about the subject of psychic phenomena. As for mediumship, my knowledge of the spirit people centered on the dangers rumored to be inherent in playing with a Ouija board. So I began to educate myself; for the next 10 years I read what I could find on the subjects of spirit people, psychic abilities, reincarnation and the process of dying. I took seminars, workshops, and classes, some of which were truly eye-opening, and many of which were just plain ridiculous. I learned about runes, pendulums, crystal balls, tarot cards, and scrying. I studied hypnosis and the power of the subconscious mind. I met some great teachers and some obvious fakes. And then I reached a saturation point: I was either capable or incapable. I was either able to control my psychic mediumship ability or I wasn't. It all came down to a decision.

Yes, you read that right. After all that learning and reading and listening, I knew that if I was going to exercise control of my psychic abilities I had to take control of them. I decided right then that I was going to stop gathering information and start using it. I simply decided that *I could do* what I'd been reading about, and I set out to prove it to myself. The decision point came very early one August morning. I'd recently purchased a house north of New York City and had been living there only a few months when I got up to use the restroom at about 3:00 a.m. Half-asleep, I looked to my right out the open door, and saw two pilots standing in the living room. Seeing spirit people randomly pop up all over the place was one thing; being watched on the john was just taking it too far. I slammed the door and muttered to myself, "I've got to start setting the rules here."

You might be wondering exactly what I mean when I say I "saw" two pilots. Right now, take a look at something on your desk or in the room. Look for a moment, then close your eyes. You can still see the shape or outline on the inside of your eyelids, correct? This is the way a clairvoyant vision appears to me. Sometimes what I see resembles a faint chalk sketch on a blackboard; very subtle, and such that if you look right at it, it disappears. Looking with your peripheral vision or your mind's eye eliminates the competition from the actual physical sense of sight, which easily overpowers the subtle picture.

The decision was therefore made, and, as if by magic, I found work at the New York Renaissance Faire as a psychic. What a training ground that turned out to be! Sure, it was nerve-wracking in the beginning, but what did I have to lose? Most of the Faire-goers were a couple of pints of mead shy of a coma by the time they made it down Mystic Way for a reading, and I'd never see them again in my life. It was during these six weekends that I realized I was indeed a very capable, accurate psychic medium, and my confidence soared. As my confidence increased, my accuracy did as well. No matter what you're doing, if you're practicing a skill you are going to improve.

Since then I've given readings on my own weekly call-in radio show, as a guest on shows hosted by others, at psychic fairs, spiritualist church services, in public, and privately. I've contributed accurate information in the search for a missing person. I've had fabulous, extraordinary, amazing spirit communications, and some that were rather average—but a spirit person has attended every single reading or message circle I've ever given, and conveyed something personal and touching, if not profound, to the loved ones who came looking for them.

CHAPTER 2

How Do We Communicate With Spirits?

When I tell people that anyone can communicate with spirit people, most of them shudder and say, "Oh, I'd be too scared." I always come back with this: if you're scared, you're not having a psychic or mediumistic experience—you're just freaking yourself out! I'll be the first to admit, being startled by pilots in the living room while half-asleep on the toilet can be a bit unnerving, but it's by no means scary. The spirit people and their mode of communication are just too subtle. Your own emotions and common sense are more powerful and can easily override the information that your sixth sense is noticing.

For clarification, the words *psychic* and *medium* mean two different things, though generally the skills go hand in hand.

A *psychic* uses the information in the energy of physical things to tell you about the physical world. The psychic is able to quiet down the information coming in from the five physical senses and concentrate on what the sixth sense is offering about a voice, a room, an object, a photograph, a piece of jewelry, and so forth. This process is called psychometry.

A *medium* uses information communicated from a spirit person, a human being who has since passed away, to tell you about the physical world or the spirit world. The medium also quiets down the stimuli from the physical senses and concentrates on the impressions he or she is feeling from a spirit.

At the end of this book you'll find plenty of exercises to develop your own psychic abilities and spirit communication skills. They're all safe and easy, and your confidence will soar as you meet with regular validation. I know the exercises work because I've used them all myself and regularly teach them in my Developing Spirit Communication classes. You'll also find ordering information for additional books I've written, as well as self-hypnosis audio files I've created, to further enhance your abilities. Please try them all out, and stick with the exercises that work best for you. Remember, I have gleaned these techniques from over ten years of research, and not all will resonate with every individual.

How It Feels To Tune In

So what does it feel like for a spirit person to visit you, if it isn't scary? For those who are developing their skills and even for me now with certain spirit people, the ability to concentrate is paramount. I used to go through a short visual exercise before any reading, where I would imagine diving deep into cool, clear water. If you've ever been underwater, it seems as though the outside world just gets quieter and dimmer. I would imagine that and then pay attention to the feelings that came after. I sometimes say a rosary or other repetitive prayer to relax the busy conscious mind and get into a mentally relaxed trance state. Nowadays, I do a breathing meditation right before my client arrives. This is just a short exercise that signals my physical senses to recede and my sixth sense to come forward. Whatever you choose to do, be sure to stick with it for a while so you can condition your body and conscious mind to relax pretty quickly on cue.

Even though my strongest learning style is not auditory, I'll use a music metaphor to illustrate how it feels to concentrate and tune into the spirit people.

Imagine you know nothing about classical music, yet it plays in the background of your office or in the market where you shop. You may occasionally hear something in the music that is particularly delightful or jarring, which stands out somehow. Think of the ongoing current of psychic information and spirit communication like that. What manages to make it through the busy thoughts, noises, and work of the day is something either remarkably pleasant or remarkably edgy.

Now imagine you've decided you're going to listen with attention to a certain piece of music from beginning to end. You'll probably set aside a quiet time and place, get comfortable, and begin concentrating on the music. You control the experience, including when to start, what the volume should be, and whether you want to rewind certain parts of it. Let's take this analogy a little bit further. Imagine, while you're listening, that you're only going to listen for a certain instrument, like the cello. You have to concentrate, focus, and listen or tune in very closely.

For someone who works as a psychic medium, this is similar to the effort we go through and what the experience is like, though it gets easier with practice. The more you listen to music, the easier it becomes to pick out the cello, timpani, or clarinet. With enough practice, you can hear and distinguish several instruments at once. For mediums, this is a valuable skill as spirit people often come in a rush and vie for my attention.

The Five "Clairs"

Every one of us is born with the sixth sense. We all have intuition, hunches, gut feelings, instincts and inspirations. In my estimation, at least ninety-five percent of the population has experienced something out of the ordinary, paranormal, or a little too eerie to be mere coincidence. These moments are totally random for most people who aren't practicing psychic mediums. They may feel as though they see or hear something they can't quite pin down, or they might just get a funny feeling urging them to do or not do something.

I believe five extra senses that mimic our physical senses make up our sixth sense:

Clairvoyance	the impression of seeing with the mind's eye
Clairaudience	the impression of a sound in the mind's ear
Clairsentience	the awareness of an impression or knowledge that pops in unexpectedly; it can also mean a feeling on the skin, like a touch or breeze, or a change in temperature
Clairgustience	the impression of tasting
Clairscent	the impression of smelling

A fairly new term, *claircognizance,* has been coined to explain knowing without logical reason. In my years of study that has been explained by the term *clairsentience*, which is the term I'll continue to use throughout this book.

Our sixth sense usually conveys subtle information to us primarily through one of these first three major extra-senses. The other two, *clairgustience* and *clairscent*, tend to play a supporting role and are more likely to come in when the spirit person wants to convey additional detail.

We all have different learning styles that are easiest for us, and it makes sense that our sixth sense would also mirror those strengths. A learning style refers to the three main sensory receivers—visual, auditory, and kinesthetic—to determine a person's preference or facility for perceiving and remembering information. A person who understands directions most effectively by listening to instructions rather than reading them, would most likely rate higher in the auditory channel than the visual.

For example, I score the highest number in the kinesthetic channel, followed by the visual channel. My auditory score is low. It is no surprise therefore that I'm mostly clairsentient and secondarily clairvoyant. I'm almost never clairaudient. I very rarely hear a spirit's voice or hear his message. The spirit person will usually give me a feeling and then a picture. It used to make me crazy that I couldn't hear the spirit people, and I spent a long time working on developing this skill and met with only moderate success. As a result, I really struggled with confidence in my abilities. I finally realized I was getting the information anyway through feelings and images. There was no reason add tension to a situation in which I was supposed to be relaxed, by forcing myself to try to hear.

I recommend that all my students figure out what communication channel is most natural, and stick with it. Don't fight your own natural tendencies. The spirit people will find a way to get their message through one channel or another. If a spirit person wants me to know his name, instead of saying it, he might show me the face of a celebrity with the same name, he might spell it out, or he might just give me the urge to say it.

Tests for determining your learning style are called VAK (visual/auditory/kinesthetic) learning style questionnaires. You can find them on the web, or simply use the one I've included in Chapter 19. Understanding your natural style increases confidence, so I recommend taking a VAK questionnaire if you're practicing your psychic abilities.

The Setting

I give individual readings and conduct both private and open message circles regularly in my home. One person arranges and brings a group of family or friends with him to a private message circle. Seats in an open message circle are available on a first-come, first-serve basis. Because I offer them at set times and dates throughout the month, interested guests can sign up in advance to attend. In open message circles, most of the guests have never met each other, unless a couple of friends come together.

When I'm preparing for a message circle in my home, I feel the spirit people begin to assemble. I may be vacuuming and feel like I've run into a person. It seems so clear to me that I usually blurt out, "Excuse me!" While I'm eating lunch or writing, they'll often pop in to say, "I'm going to be here later. Remember, I had a stroke when I was pregnant and went out that way." This used to get quite annoying. If I were trying to concentrate on what groceries I needed, I found it impossible to focus on my list while so many spirits were trying to get my attention. I found myself shooing them away so often as I tried to get ready for the evening that I had to set up some ground rules:

- All spirit people are welcome to assemble in advance of a message circle, but they are to wait on the porch
- No interrupting me during the day
- No popping in while I'm working with other clients
- Take turns during the message circle. I promise I will get to you

They seem as excited as the physical people anticipating a reunion. When I step out onto the porch, the air seems to pop around me like popcorn. I feel like I've walked into a crowded gathering where the people started partying long before I arrived. My office is on the porch, so I've given up trying to get any writing done on the day of a circle. I couldn't even work on this book on circle days, due to all the activity. I always know in advance when a circle will be unexpectedly called off at the last minute. It's either because no spirit people show up during the day or the energy building on my porch suddenly dissolves. It's like the noisy crowd in the next room vanishes in an instant.

As the guests gather in my living room, I crack the door to my porch open a few inches. Even though I almost never tell anyone why, at nearly every circle a guest says, "Is someone on your porch? I see something moving out there;" or "Is there another person out on your porch? I hear noises." I only tell them after the circle that they are experiencing clairvoyance or clairaudience themselves!

For private readings that are one-on-one, the preparation process is the same, and my clients often comment on movement or sounds they notice behind the porch door. By the way, whenever I do private readings or message circles, I ask my spirit guides to help me, and I have trained my subconscious mind to forget everything about my clients. I have had people return to my house whom I swear I have never met before, yet they claim to have been at my home for readings. I ask to erase my memory because, if a client or guest should return, I want to make sure I am using my mediumship and psychic ability, and not my memory, to bring in details for them about lost loved ones.

Piggy-backing

The spirit people taught me something a few years ago that I call piggy-backing. One seems to draft in behind a previous spirit with whom she has something in common, and, once the first spirit has been validated, will nudge him out of the way and announce, "Everything he said, and this other detail."

The first time this happened I was giving a message circle that was comprised of fourteen people. Most of them did not know each other. At one point, a grandmother in spirit came in. She showed herself to be obese, diabetic, and Polish. I felt pulled in three directions with the spirit so I indicated three areas of the circle and asked everyone to pay attention. I didn't know where I was going with her at first.

When I described her, three separate people, strangers to each other, raised their hands to indicate she belonged to them. When I began to talk about an art deco lamp left behind, Marge nodded while Ellen and Delia shook their heads. The spirit lady then said,

"You picked out my dress and kept my rosary after the funeral service." Ellen nodded her head while Marge and Delia shook theirs. Finally the spirit gave another detail about a family cat, which Delia delightedly confirmed, while Marge and Ellen couldn't connect. Marge, Ellen, and Delia did not know each other in life, nor did their grandmothers know each other. The spirits took the most efficient way to communicate by coming in together, and then took turns announcing their individual identities with personal details.

Quite often a guest will be validating a spirit person as belonging to them, when I'll suddenly feel the need to jump over to another guest. I've since come to understand it's because the spirit I've been describing to the first guest has something in common with the spirit who comes in next, even though the physical people present and the spirit people have never met one another. When I've brought in the next spirit person and gotten validation, the connecting piggyback thread becomes clear. They may both have had the same first name, drank martinis, suffered from the same illness, and so on.

It's fascinating to see how the spirit people queue up because I never know in advance how a spirit communication will go. I was conducting a private message circle in my home recently that was made up of two women and one man. The first spirit to come through for one of the women in the group was a young man named Lou. He told me he would be acting in the spirit world like a traffic cop, letting spirits through one at a time and stopping others. He gave me the sense that he was timing the spirit people.

Lou was joking lightly about himself and my guest when he prompted me to ask her, "Were you the weird kid in the group?"

"I think we both were," she answered.

"He keeps bringing it up and laughing about it, and he shows me your wrist, he keeps indicating the wrist. Did he leave you a watch or did you just do something to your wrist?"

"I just got a tattoo on my wrist after he died." She showed me the stars tattooed on her wrist.

To more conservative folks, I guess that would be kind of weird. Lou had passed away just a few weeks before, and my guest felt so delighted to hear from her friend.

"Is there a Rob or a Bob that he knows?"

"Well, sort of. He was friends with a Rob's daughter."

I didn't really feel as though that's who Lou was indicating, so I tuned back in for a little more information. "I feel like he's introducing somebody else, like he's wheeled in someone in a wheelchair." I indicated to my guest and the woman seated next to her. "Both of you please listen because I sense I'm being pulled over here. I feel like this person looks sort of unkempt, sitting here with his head down. I'm getting the feeling that the person is really mentally not there. Not because of drugs, but because of old age, dementia, or some mental disconnect. He either looks really old, or he is really old. He looks like a very frail or very old person. Either his disease has aged him a lot, or he is really very old."

The other woman seated in the group said, "Oh, that's for me, that's my Bob!"

We were able to continue with the message from Bob. As soon as that message was over, Lou stepped right back in as a sort of master of ceremonies and ushered out Bob and brought the next spirit person in.

The Language of Spirit People

The frequent act of communicating with the spirit people naturally creates a shorthand or language of its own, and that shorthand is the use of symbols. Symbols carry so much more information than a word, and, through the frequent exposure to these symbols, the spirits and I have created a kind of library or vocabulary in my mind. For instance, when a spirit person wants to say happy birthday to a child, he'll show me balloons. If it's an adult's birthday, he comes in with what looks like a box with a bow on it. For the birthday of a young friend or peer, the spirit will show me one of those toy horns we toot at celebrations. These small refinements have become familiar to me over the years, and having an ever-expanding symbol vocabulary available to both the spirit people and me allows for quite detailed communication.

Spirit people also indicate to me that I'm on the right track or that the guest or client has properly identified them by giving me a kind of *zing!* up my spine. Quite often, loved ones have passed from the same thing, or the guest isn't quite sure because my description could signify more than one person in spirit. As we exchange more information from the spirit world, when the client or guest believes she can identify the spirit and says so, I'll get that bright, buzzing current up my spine, and I can say, "Yes, this is who we're talking to." At that point, the spirit will usually be able to give many more details about himself once he has been recognized.

When a spirit person wants to define his illness or what caused his passing, he'll usually give me a feeling as if I am experiencing it, too. For someone with heart trouble, I'll feel a fluttering in my heart. If it's heart disease that runs in the family, I'll also get a symbol of a DNA spiral. I feel a sharp pop in my head if the spirit person wants to indicate a stroke or aneurysm, which is a distinct feeling from an impact that happens outside the skull, such as in a car accident or mugging. I have felt tuberculosis, amputation, gunshot wounds, being hit by a train, jumping off a bridge, schizophrenia, Alzheimer's, and confusion due to drugs or alcohol. I've never experienced any of those things in reality, but, using a combination of feelings and symbols, I'm able to convey the spirit's physical and mental condition.

I usually get the cause of death from a spirit person first, and then a tug toward one guest or another if we're in a circle. It's important to note that the spirit isn't still suffering from these conditions, but is simply using it as a way to identify himself. The feeling associated with the cause of death will persist until the client validates, at which point the feeling disappears. I know the client isn't connecting my information with the right spirit if the feeling I have persists, so I'll ask the spirit for more detailed information. I will have the feeling of my head exploding in a stroke until we identify that spirit, so I am very eager to get the spirit connected to his loved one seated somewhere around me.

This happened not too long ago in a private circle in my home. One of the first spirits to come in announced her death by uterine cancer and gave me several other details as well. My guest couldn't identify her, and, for the remainder of the circle, I felt this terrible ache of uterine cancer and continued to return to the original guest without any success. Finally, toward the end, when I couldn't stand it anymore, I begged this spirit woman to give me just one more thing, whatever my guest needed.

"Who is Anna or Ann?" I asked the guest.

"Oh my God, it's my mother-in-law, Anna! She died from uterine cancer. I don't know why I didn't think of her." Relief at last.

The Chimney

When I lead message circles, one spot, or sometimes one person, can act as a connecting point with the spirit world. I call this connecting point the chimney. In my house it's a section of the couch in the corner opposite the porch door. The chimney seems to be the conduit where all the spirits land when they begin to come in. They appear there first, and then pull me over to the person they've come to see. When there is a spirit guide or spirit person who is acting as a medium in their world, they often stay in the chimney. Lou, the spirit man who acted as the traffic cop I mentioned earlier, spent the whole circle in that corner, ushering the spirits in and out.

When the chimney is a person, I feel like I want to give every spirit who comes in to that person. Every spirit who comes in either stands by that person or pulls me towards him or her. After two or three attempts to connect the spirit with the chimney guest, I ask the guests in the rest of the circle if they can identify the spirit. Someone usually does, I deliver the message, and once again return to the chimney guest to begin bringing through the next spirit. I can tell after a few minutes if we have a chimney guest or chimney spot in a room, and explain to all the guests that they'll all have to listen to help me identify which spirit belongs to which guest.

When families come together, it's as if the chimney effect has multiplied. I always ask during open circles if there are family members present. If so, I can prepare the rest of the guests for another unique experience.

A few years ago I was conducting an open circle comprised of twelve people. I hadn't met any of the guests before, except for one woman, Marie. Our evening progressed beautifully, though I found out in short order that I had three siblings sitting together. Marie had brought her sisters.

Usually when family energy is present, it's their spirit people who come through first and stay the longest. Because I guarantee everyone will get a message, I often have to ask the family's spirits to step aside for a bit so I can bring in other guests' loved ones. On this particular evening, I spent almost half an hour bringing in Marie's spirit people. It was time to give someone else a chance. I asked silently for spirit people not related to Marie and her sisters, and I was pulled over to an older female guest.

"I have a male spirit here who is showing me that he was in the service in World War II. He looks a bit like Clark Gable, very handsome and debonair."

My guest answered that she couldn't connect right away, so I continued.

"He was stationed in the Marshall Islands for a while, and used to send home souvenirs from there, things made with coconuts and shells."

She still had trouble connecting, so I asked the spirit man for something unmistakably specific. "He fathered a child with a woman who lived there. When he came home to his wife and family he had to send money there."

Nope.

"He loved horses and was often at the track."

No idea.

"You have a picture of him in his khaki uniform, which he always used to bring out. He talked alot about how much he loved the islands."

I could practically hear crickets now as my guest continued to give me a blank stare. Could I be totally bombing with this lady?

"He was often drinking cocktails, he has an unusual name that begins with an M, like 'Murray' or something."

Silence.

Then I see a tentative hand slowly come up from Marie on the other side of the room. Those details exactly matched an uncle in her family. Aha! I tuned in again to the spirit who was exuding mirth and mischief. He told me he hadn't been brought in yet when I asked the sisters' spirit people to step aside. He didn't want to miss an opportunity to come in, so he stood in front of someone else and pretended to belong to her. The sisters agreed: that was exactly the sort of trick he'd pull while still in a physical body.

The spirit people teach me something new every day!

Spirit Guides

People often ask me about the presence of spirit guides, and I can honestly say I don't have many answers. I rarely bring them through in private readings or circles, because I feel it's my job as a medium to connect my guests with a spirit they can identify. Otherwise, why bother? Since the existence of a spirit guide cannot be proven or validated, my clients wouldn't be getting what they paid for if I didn't give them details, names, identifying characteristics and other evidence that would absolutely convince them that their loved ones carry on living and loving them.

When clients ask me specifically to tune into a spirit guide, I will do so, but I usually like to show my clients how to discover this guide for themselves. On occasions when I have brought in spirit guides, my clients have said "Yes, other mediums told me about him," or "I saw the same woman in my meditation." In Chapter 20 you'll find a wonderful meditation to help you connect with your own team of guides on the other side.

I have been aware of different guides at different times in my life. When I began to practice as a psychic medium professionally, I specifically asked for the presence of a spirit guide during my meditations. I saw a young native American male, who said he was guiding me in this process. My first reaction? "Yeah, right!" Why is it that everyone has a native American spirit guide? Is it some sort of mass hypnosis by the New Age industry? I started asking for a real guide instead, but this same guide continued to appear. Only after a much-respected medium mentioned to me in passing, "You have a very handsome native American male spirit standing behind you," did I decide to take whatever guidance I could get and stop worrying about how New Age-y it seemed.

I don't know this guide's name, but he always made his presence known by creating a tingling across the bridge of my nose or by showing me what looked like a trout swimming, its silvery sides flashing in the bright water. These were such bizarre impressions that I knew I wasn't imagining them. Whenever I got them, I knew to pay attention either to what I had just done or what I was about to do.

For several years this spirit guided me in developing my skills and my business. About five years ago I began to see him less and less, and for a while it seemed I had no guides at all. More recently, I've become aware of a group of guides who appear to stand around me in a semi-circle when I meditate. I call them the council. The leader always wears a hooded brown robe. I don't hear his voice nor yet understand the directions he gives me, but I can feel a bright energy when he lays his hands on top of my head.

Spirit guides may or may not exist. I never used to believe in them, but now I do, and I take advantage of their wisdom and assistance, particularly when I'm working with spirit communication. Before appointments or circles I ask my guides, whoever they may be, to help me turn down the volume on my physical senses and to help prepare my mind for the subtle impressions of spirit people.

Anyone can say that we have certain guides around us, but I feel it's important to meet them yourself. It's also my personal experience that guides change as we do, so having someone tell you about a guide when you're in your twenties doesn't mean that guide is still around you in your fifties. Many good meditations and other sources are available if you want to discover your own spirit guides. Search the web or start with some of the resources listed at the end of this book.

A common question from my clients has to do with whether their loved ones in spirit act as guides or not. The spirit people tell me that they can't interfere with a person's free will, and they can't necessarily see the future. When I ask them, the spirit people talk about things they can see within a rather narrow window of time, either the immediate past, the present, or the immediate future. So while they may not act as guides steering us towards better decisions, they have told me they can bring healing energy or influence their loved ones in the physical world in a few ways.

A man had come to see me for a reading, and I immediately brought in his father, who my client had felt around his house. We talked with his dad for a little while, and then my client's mother came through. She had very little to say, but she kept showing me that she was holding her hands over my client's wife's heart. She told me she was praying for and sending healing energy to her daughter-in-law. My client told me tearfully that his wife had just had open heart surgery, and he was very worried about her recovery. Knowing his mother was guiding her healing brought him great peace. He couldn't wait to go home and tell his wife, who had been close to his mother.

In a different reading, the mother of a guest came through and showed me that she was on a bus. When I conveyed this perplexing information to the client, she exclaimed that on that very day something amazing had happened. She had been thinking mournfully about her mother while waiting to cross the street, and looked up just as a bus was passing. On the bus was an ad for Miriam Hospital. Her grief vanished in an instant and she found herself smiling with joy, because Miriam was her mother's name. This feels like guidance of a sort, when a spirit sees our situation and influences us to notice something.

PART TWO

Common Questions

CHAPTER 3

Do You Have To Believe To Get A Message?

When I first started to practice as a psychic medium, I had the unique experience of working at the New York Renaissance Faire. Amy let me share her site for six weekends in August and September. In return, I would pay her a percentage of what I made during the day.

I wasn't the first psychic Amy had hired. She had gotten into a battle of wills with my predecessor, and the psychic abruptly quit. During our interview, Amy told me in a stage whisper that the psychic "had darkness all around her." She went on to describe her primitive nature and even threw in words like "voodoo" and "exotic." A picture began to form of Amy's personality, but I was excited about the prospect of earning money for what I loved to do. I just focused on the dollar signs floating before my eyes.

To be fair, Amy had suffered a traumatic brain injury years before and wasn't capable of focusing or working for long stretches. And while I hadn't known her before the brain injury, it was pretty clear that it had affected her personality. What I mean is that most of the time she was a lovely, dreamy, sweet and flaky sort of lady, very charming and sincere. Suddenly though, completely unprovoked, she would go into a totally inappropriate rage.

I remember returning from a lunch break with my guy, and being ambushed by Amy. She leapt out from behind her display shouting at me at the top of her lungs. "Where have you been? Don't you know there's work to do? People have been looking for readings from you, and I had to tell them to come back!"

I said, "My Heavens, it's a huge fairgrounds, I'm certain that whoever was looking for me found some way to entertain themselves for half an hour." Then she turned her rage on my poor sweetheart, who, caught completely off-guard by her outrage, stood rooted to the spot while she berated him.

At other times Amy would sidle up to me while showering me with compliments and affection. When there was no one sitting at my table or waiting for a reading, she would run over, sit down, and say, "Tell me what you see for me. Am I on the right path? Will I travel? Will I get money from somewhere? Do you see my spirit guides?" Endless, repeated questions of exactly the same nature.

This sort of obsequious manner is at first rather flattering. Who wouldn't feel a glow under the devoted attention of someone who thinks you're really gifted? Especially a new psychic like me. An established practitioner was praising me and seeking my insights. Heck, I must be really good at this! Amy would literally eat up my time at the table, shooing away paying customers so she could analyze every nuance of every impression I conveyed.

At the end of the Faire I'd earned far less than I'd envisioned, thanks to Amy, but I learned four priceless lessons:

- Set clear boundaries with clients; it's up to me to end a reading
- Take charge of the reading right from the beginning, to set the tone and pace
- Communicate the time and cost clearly with the client
- Read the client before giving him a reading

The last lesson might sound peculiar, but it was one I had to learn the hard way. One early afternoon, while enduring another endless round of Amy's questions, I became aware of a young man observing us and waiting for a turn. I ousted Amy from the chair and invited him to sit down. The details of our reading have faded with time, but he was very satisfied when we were done, and left to go find his fiancée. When he returned with her, I expected an enthusiastic guest and another easy $25. Instead, he literally dragged her up to my table. Her arms were crossed defensively and she had a hostile glare on her pretty face.

She said, "I don't believe in this. I don't want to do it."

He kept insisting she would love it, it was really cool, it would blow her mind; she kept refusing, rejecting, and shaking her head. Finally she sat down, stared at me, and said, "Well?"

The first spirit to come in was one who hadn't quite made it into the world, due to either abortion or miscarriage. So, in the service of this spirit, I announced its presence.

"I don't know what you're talking about. You're completely wrong," was her reply.

Oh, okay. It's possible I'm wrong. Attempting to move on, I looked around in my mind for other spirit people. When I became aware of a few and asked them to come forward, they sent the little fetal spirit forward again. It seemed like they were waiting in a half circle just out of sight, or reach, or definition. When they put the little spirit forward again, it was as if they were saying to me, "Deal with this one first, she's important, then we'll come through."

"I'm sorry to insist," I said, "and you don't need to confirm or deny to me, but I still need to talk about this little spirit." I let her know she needn't validate, as some people don't want others hearing or knowing that they didn't complete a pregnancy for whatever reason. Furthermore, we were not in a very private place at the Faire.

I didn't hear anything in reply, and after a moment I opened my eyes. When I did, her face was not six inches from mine as she leaned across the table.

"I told you: YOU. ARE. WRONG," she hissed through gritted teeth. "If you do not give me my money back right now, I'm going to your boss. Give me back my money. You are a fraud."

I complied right away, of course. About half an hour later her fiancé came back and sat down across from me. He apologized for her, and asked what had happened. When I told him the details of our very brief reading, he told me she'd miscarried several months ago and was still very upset about it.

After he left, I wondered why the spirit people hadn't sent forward someone she might have accepted, maybe a beloved aunt or childhood pet. I felt that I had failed them as well as the young woman, but when I asked, her spirit people assured me that she had to hear from this little child. They told me her anger about this miscarriage was so great that she couldn't see anything until she could see that. They wanted to tell her that nothing was lost, no one had died, and in time the same little spirit would return to her. The spirit people wanted this young woman to forgive herself, and to open up her heart to the future again, because if she stayed focused on this anger and grief she would not be able to be the person who could bring the spirit back in.

I tell this story because it happened early in my professional career, and had an enormous impact on how I work. If I had read that client correctly—read her body language and listened to what she was saying—I would never have given her a psychic reading at all. She told me right at the beginning that she was not an appropriate client, and neither I nor her fiancé listened to her. As a result, my confidence was shaken and she was made upset.

Hearing From A Spirit

Everyone is capable of getting a message from a spirit person they know. I believe the spirit people are always willing to show up and say hello. What's really necessary is for the physical person to have a willingness to show up also. The answer to this chapter's question is, yes, you have to believe in mediumship to hear a message. Before you can accept a message from a spirit person, you have to be open to the possibility of spirit communication.

Imagine you were traveling in a foreign land, learning all sorts of amazing things. If you had the opportunity to call home to tell the folks there how really great it was, wouldn't you be eager to share the news? Sure you would. That is, if the folks back home would actually pick up the receiver and listen to you. You might get a couple of family members on the phone, but let's say one or two would adamantly refuse to talk to you, because they didn't believe you were actually there. They couldn't believe it was you speaking because they couldn't see you in person. The fact that it had to come through a telephone rendered evidence of your experience completely immaterial. The telephone could convey your warmth, personality, and voice without judgment, yet if the person on the other end of the line refused to believe it was you, no amount of evidence would suffice.

I think of myself as that telephone. The messages don't originate from me. I'm simply the conduit for the information. Another way to think of a medium is as a translator. Let's say you're hearing someone speaking French, and you don't have any familiarity with that language. If you're interested in what the French-speaking person is saying, you need someone who does speak that language to listen to the French words, and then translate them into your language, let's say English. The key, of course, is the word, "if." If you're not interested in hearing what the French person has to say, you wouldn't seek out a translator. Even if someone were to drag you up to one and force you to sit and listen, if you had a particular prejudice against French-speaking people or didn't believe French people actually existed, nothing the translator told you would matter.

A common question that comes up during message circles or private readings is, "Can my spirit person hear me?" Or sometimes, "Can I ask the spirit person a question?" Absolutely! Ask away! You don't need a medium to translate your question to the spirit person. To continue with our translator metaphor, imagine that the French-speaking person understands English perfectly, but can't speak it.

For a long time, as I was building my practice and my reputation, there always seemed to be one person in a message circle who didn't want to be there. That was truly puzzling to me. I always wanted to ask those resistant clients, "You've paid good money to connect with someone in spirit. Why aren't you open to hearing from them?"

As my reputation has grown this problem has diminished greatly, yet from time to time I still get one of these individuals. As recently as six months ago, a friend of mine brought her eighty-something year old mother to an open circle, with about twelve others in attendance. I began to get spirit people for this mother almost immediately, and I eagerly shared their details. I got nothing back. Not a nod, not a "yes," nor even a "could be."

Spirit after spirit came through, giving names, relationships, and specific details about their personalities. I kept asking them for more, because all this elderly mother would do was shrug her shoulders and say "eh," as if she were completely unimpressed. Finally, I turned to the daughter, my friend, and I said, "Do you know any of these people?" She said, "Oh yeah, you've just named Aunt Ida, my stepfather, our childhood neighbor in Brooklyn...."

After the circle, my friend pulled me aside and said, "You know, she really doesn't believe in this stuff," and I wanted to scream, "Then why the blazes did you bring her?" Because when someone like that attends a circle, it drags down everyone's energy. It makes everyone else wonder, "Oh great, when Priscilla gets to me, is she going to give me people I can't identify, too? Did I just waste my money? Because she's totally bombing with this person."

Validation

One of the most important things you as a guest can do either in a message circle or in a private reading, is to validate what the medium is telling you. Here's why: *No one, not even a spirit person, is going to sit around talking about themselves without any feedback or encouragement from the other person in the dialogue.*

Tuning into the spirit world is like turning on a sign over my head that says "Open For Business." When I indicate to the spirit people that I'm ready to translate for them, they step forward (and not always politely taking turns, either; they often interrupt each other or nudge each other out of the way). I wait to get several feelings or pictures about a spirit, then share those details with the client. If the client indicates that she knows, or thinks she knows, who I'm talking about, the incoming information from the spirit person ramps up in frequency, vibration, and speed. Once we've made a connection, the spirit person and I, a huge flood of information follows.

Recall our telephone metaphor, and consider a conversation with a beloved grandmother you haven't seen in years. The spirit person is calling, the phone's ringing, and you, the guest, pick up. "This is your grandmother," the spirit person might say. "Grandma, is that really you?" would be your excited response. A connection! The spirit person joyfully understands that you recognize her, and suddenly she just can't talk fast enough, because she has so much to say.

But if you, the guest, refuse to acknowledge the spirit person because you're testing the medium, you are bound to lose the connection. Let's replay that phone metaphor:

"This is your grandmother," conveys the spirit person.

You don't respond.

"I was sick with leukemia before I came out here."

You still don't respond.

"You and your mother picked out the blue dress I was waked in, and she gave you my rosary after the service."

Still nothing from you.

"Your grandfather Bob is here with me. He is happy that you smoke his brand of cigar every year on his birthday."

You are still silent.

...and Grandmother backs away so another spirit person can step forward for someone else in the group.

I'm not asking you to accept every vague thing a medium says. A healthy dose of skepticism will probably make your experience much more enjoyable, as you're likely to experience a whole new level of faith by the time you leave. Every medium should give you relevant, detailed evidence from your spirit person that he or she couldn't make up, and not just platitudes like "I see a nurturing figure here who gives you lots of love." But help the medium make the connection by participating in the dialogue. It's only going to allow more information to come through. A medium may ask you a specific question about the spirit person, such as a name, but an ethical medium will not fish for information. Recognize the difference. I will only ask a specific question once I've connected the spirit person with the guest. It will help me to connect more deeply with the spirit, which allows for even more evidence to come through.

In the process of conveying that detailed, specific information to you from a spirit person, remember that the medium has to translate or interpret what the spirit person is saying. Spirit people often give their messages in the form of symbols, because symbols can convey so much more than a sentence. Nuances can be lost or missed in that translation process, so expect some leeway. I've noticed that as the spirit connection warms up, more specific information comes through more quickly. Don't be surprised if a medium speaks slowly or vaguely when first connecting with a spirit. She's just learning that spirit's dialect. Validate if you understand who she's brought through, and as that connection warms up, you'll be treated to even more amazing evidence.

I once brought in a fiery-haired female spirit. This spirit came through very strongly, and as I stammered through my opening connection with her, I used the word "Celtic" to describe her ethnicity. Then more detail followed: She was a grandmother; had passed well before her time; had long, bright red, wavy hair; played the harp; was a published poet; had been married three times; and recognized that the guest she belonged to had just given birth to twins. The guest kept saying, "No" to everything I said. In the end, I gave up on this spirit, assuming I'd been mistaken. At the end of the circle this particular guest came up to me and said, "You were describing my grandmother perfectly, but you said 'Celtic' and she was Scottish."

We mediums will be as specific as we can be, but remember, we're still translating from one language to another. If we get close, give us some encouragement. You don't have to say "yes," but please, don't say "no"—especially if *every other single detail* describes your grandmother! Some nuances will likely be lost in the translation, but if the overall picture defines your spirit person, admit it. I wanted to give this woman a message from her grandmother, but she got hung up on this one small detail, and so the opportunity was lost.

Skepticism

I believe every person who is open to hearing from someone no longer in physical form, can get a message from a spirit. Do you have to believe completely? I don't know if any of us can ever completely believe in something not immediately tangible. I don't know if our rational minds can ever wholly accept something non-rational. But if you're willing to participate in a reading by not testing the medium, and by acknowledging evidence, a truly wonderful experience awaits.

However, if you don't believe, don't even bother. Avoid wasting your money and the medium's time. If someone has to drag you to a circle or a reading, and you're convinced it's all bunk, you're absolutely not going to hear from a spirit. The spirit people don't need to convince you. You'll be there soon enough to see for yourself. Many spirits have come through acknowledging that they didn't believe in the spirit world when they were alive, either.

I did a reading for a young woman whose father came through with details about his work, his nickname for her, and all sorts of wonderful evidence she could validate. He finished up his message by kidding her about getting a reading. If he were alive he would have given her a hard time about seeing a medium, because he "didn't believe in that horse shit." It was a phrase he'd often used to describe anything he thought was bunk, including the afterlife. My client left knowing she had indeed been visiting with her dad.

I remember one message circle a few years ago. The women in the family had come before, but this time they brought one of the husbands. Bill was a healthy skeptic—my favorite kind of guest. They come in wanting and needing proof, but are willing to accept it when it's given. It is pure joy to watch that skepticism melt away as they are presented with details from their loved ones in spirit that they simply can't deny. They usually leave on a total high, shaking their heads in disbelief, laughing, relieved, hopeful, and happy.

Bill sat on my left, his chair pushed a little bit out of the fairly even circle described by the other chairs. He wasn't quite into it with the group. Yet he was leaning forward in the chair, and his chair position and body language described his inner conflict over the validity of what he was about to experience. Hopeful, excited, and willing to be convinced—yes; but rational and skeptical as well.

The spirit people seem to like these guys the best, too, because I almost always find myself beginning with them. Right away an uncle came through for Bill. He showed me opening his shirt and exposing a scar, like his chest had been cracked for heart surgery. He was laughing about it. This wasn't a traumatic surgery that killed him. The look on Bill's face told me this circle was going to be a blast. He admitted right away that when he was younger, his Uncle Harry used to open his shirt at family gatherings to show off his heart surgery scar, just to gross out the ladies and the kids. I went to Harry and I asked him for one more detail, one precious, perfect idea that I could share with Bill that would win him over forever. Harry showed me, and I conveyed to Bill, that he was now "bowling with the angels."

When Bill stopped laughing, crying and shouting all at once, he said that when he was a little boy and afraid during electrical storms, Uncle Harry used to explain that there was nothing to fear, because thunder was really just angels bowling up in heaven. Bill had forgotten all about that many years ago, yet here was Harry, not only reassuring Bill with a special detail from his childhood, but also giving us all an idea of where he was and what he was doing.

Several other spirits came through during the rest of that evening's circle, but Harry stayed in the room the whole time. In between the other spirits he'd pop up with some other funny anecdote. At the end of the evening I practically had to send Harry away, and it was the same with Bill. He kept shaking my hand and smiling from ear to ear. Bill also acknowledged that Harry was still very much like himself when he was alive—always telling funny stories and commanding attention from the center of the room.

CHAPTER 4

Are They Always Around Us, Watching?

Many of my clients express absolute delight that their loved ones in spirit are still participating in family life. The spirit people show up with birthday presents to acknowledge a client's birthday, comment on meals that are being cooked, note visits to the dentist, or even the choice of new curtains hung in a baby's room. They'll lift a glass of spirit champagne if there is something to celebrate in the client's family. They go to weddings, recitals, and funerals, too.

Does that mean they're around all the time, watching us shower or argue with a spouse? Or do they anticipate our presence at a reading and only watch us right before then? It might seem like a silly question, but I've heard it so many times, I decided to go right to the source.

Besides identifying the spirit people and conveying messages, I ask each spirit person to show me something about the person they belong to. I want to show that the spirit is still participating in family life in some way. Sometimes I don't even have to ask them. A spirit person will sometimes just show up with a birthday gift or a glass of champagne. I like to share the small details, the kind that are meaningful because they seem so ordinary. A mom who passed from breast cancer showed me that she was at the store with her daughter as she chose material for curtains in her baby granddaughter's room. She liked the pattern her daughter had picked out and would be with her while she sewed, to help her keep the seams straight. The spirit mother had taught her daughter how to sew when she was a child. My guest was gratified to know that her mother was with her while she shopped, and perhaps gently influenced her choice. After her reading, she felt more deeply connected her mother, knowing she would help her teach her own baby daughter how to sew one day.

Spirit people may focus on a visit to a doctor or dentist, not only to say that he or she was there with their physical loved one, but that they had had the same thing when they were alive. One guest in a message circle was told by her dad that he was with her as she dealt with her dental issues. He'd been with her that very day when she got news of needing a root canal. He showed me a DNA spiral, which is a symbol the spirit people show me to indicate a genetic connection. This spirit was saying, "you got those bad teeth from me."

At times, the spirit people seem to have a great deal of fun teasing their physical person about what they're doing. One spirit friend came through in a private reading, and instead of giving messages, preferred to joke around about what the client was doing. He said, "You ate Chinese food last night. You got a sesame seed stuck in your teeth and kept flossing but it wouldn't come out. It bugged you all night, even while you were watching TV. In the morning you were still trying to floss it out. You know the seaweed salad always does that to you."

While my client laughed on the couch about these everyday kind of details, I found myself laughing, too. We expect such deeply profound messages from those on the other side, yet feel so much more connected to our loved ones when we know they are still talking to us in the old familiar ways.

At a circle a few years ago, the Italian mother of my guest Lorraine came through. She had been at the market while her daughter chose eggplant for the parmigiana meal earlier that evening, and had a strong opinion about her selection. She came through saying, "Why did you choose the male eggplant instead of the female eggplant? Don't you remember how bitter that gender is? Don't you remember anything I taught you about cooking?" I'm not making this up. Who even knew eggplant had gender?

Lorraine was laughing so hard, tears were streaming down her cheeks as she acknowledged that her mother would have said exactly those kinds of things. She had indeed discovered when she got home that she'd chosen the wrong eggplant.

A little later on in the circle, the spirit mother came through again, this time with a turkey baster. I felt that another round of teasing about Lorraine's cooking was about to begin, but as I waited I felt that the turkey baster was more symbolic than literal. Sure enough, in a moment I understood that the spirit mother was telling her daughter that she would soon hear about a loved one conceiving through artificial insemination. Lorraine, in her mid-fifties, couldn't imagine anyone that this would apply to, but her spirit mother just said, "You listen to me." Within two days Lorraine called me to say that a young friend had announced her pregnancy by artificial insemination.

Can They See The Future?

Clients often ask me if their loved ones in spirit can give them advice or show them the future, especially once they know the spirit is witnessing events in the present. I've been shown in individual examples and in general, that our spirit loved ones can't see too far into the future. What they are able to predict or witness falls within a very narrow window of time: the immediate past, the present, or the immediate future. We here in the physical world determine our own future trajectories, and that trajectory changes with every decision we make, no matter how minor. It is only after the fact, in hindsight, that we can see how a string of decisions lead to a certain outcome.

When John F. Kennedy, Jr. was preparing to fly himself, his wife, and her sister up to a wedding on Cape Cod in 1999, every decision he made caused him to have to make certain subsequent decisions. To illustrate, imagine you're walking and come to a fork in the road, where you cannot stop and stay still. You must decide to go left or right. Having chosen, say, the left fork, as you continue down that road you are presented with other forks, or opportunities, to go left or right. You wouldn't have a chance to make those subsequent choices if you hadn't made the first one, which was to go left. Sometimes we can go back and undo that first decision, but most times we cannot.

Every minute of our day is filled with decision-making: *Should I stay in bed another five minutes, or get up? Should I put on the air conditioner while I'm at work, or turn it off? Do I have time to read the headlines, or do I have to get right in the shower?* And it's not just actions we have to decide to do or not do. We have to decide how we feel about things: *Am I going to stay mad at my spouse? Am I going to let my frustration extend to my kids? Am I going to feel impatient waiting in traffic today, or am I just going to choose to relax and listen to music? Am I going to let the news upset me?*

These decisions may all seem inconsequential, but in hindsight we can see that they may have led to missed opportunities, or worse. Your spouse may have had just enough of your anger, and decide today that she'll ask for a divorce. Taking out your frustration on your child may be the first step that leads to a pattern of physical abuse. Your decision to remain impatient may cause you to take risks that cause a traffic accident. Or, as in the case with the Kennedy aircraft, those seemingly inconsequential decisions may lead to tragedy.

All of these decisions, no matter how minute or insignificant, map out our futures. This is free will, and the spirit people cannot interfere with it any more than a physical person can force us to do something (barring imprisonment against our will). I believe it is also for this reason that our spirit people can only show us the immediate future, or what they know we'll be doing in the next day or two. They can only see the outcome of trajectories we have already set.

Ghostly Warnings

Stories abound of people who are supernaturally warned of impending danger. A client relayed his cousin's story: After the family had gone to bed, the cousin awoke to an image of his dead mother calling his name. As he got out of bed to approach her, he smelled smoke. He ran downstairs to discover an appliance on fire. This spirit mother had insight into the immediate future, and was able to convey that to her son here on the physical plane. Yet she didn't have to ability to warn him months ago when the appliance was installed incorrectly.

Another client relates how she heard her dog barking one night. She awoke to discover someone trying to break in, and immediately called the police. When she tells this story she always waits till the end to say that her dog had died six months before.

People who engage in high-risk sports or activities experience supernatural warnings, too. They may see spirit people warning them away from a decision that, if made, could have catastrophic results. These warnings are always at the last minute, within that narrow window of time they've described to me. As a high-altitude mountaineer, I've heard many anecdotal accounts from colleagues who were warned away at the eleventh hour from routes, summits, and even partners, by spirit people. Yet those spirit people didn't show up a month before a climb to say, "Better not do that." They can't see any farther into the future than we can. We can reasonably predict the outcome of most of our actions, but we must wait to see the actual consequences of our decisions.

In my experience, and in answer to my questions, I understand that spirit people are no more powerful than we are. What they do have is a better overview of why things happened, and a more relaxed perspective on life's challenges. As they continually remind me, everything will make perfect sense when I've gone out to join them and can see for myself.

Different mediums practicing today have different ideas on the subject of whether spirit people are watching us all the time, or whether they have the ability to warn us or to influence our decisions. Personally, I don't believe the spirit people watch us at every moment. From my experience, it seems that they do anticipate the opportunity to show their loved ones that they're still active in the family, when that loved one comes to a reading or circle. It seems also that they check in with us from time to time, and attend family events or celebrations, especially when the assembled family thinks or talks about them.

In the end, it is up to the client to decide to heed warnings or follow guidance that is conveyed through a medium. As a matter of ethics and the law, I will not ever give a client advice, whether derived through a psychic impression or translated from a spirit communication. I will share what I receive in order to empower the client to make a comfortable, informed decision. Anything else improperly influences a person's right to choose freely.

CHAPTER 5

Do Spirit People Really Exist?

The conscious mind relies on input from our five physical senses.
This is the part of our mind that analyzes and solves problems, that
reasons, that uses logic, and that makes decisions. It's also the part
of the mind that gets the most attention and encouragement when
we're growing up. As a result, unless something is rational, logical, or
processed through our five physical senses, many adults don't believe
it's real.

I hope one day we'll be able to prove that spirit life continues after
death. Electricity, the automobile, and the internet were once scoffed
at by the general public, yet now most of us can't live comfortably
without them. I believe the spirit world will also become accepted as
real, eventually. In the meantime, these experiences exist outside of
the realm of proof. Many experiments have been done in controlled,
scientific environments, which suggest a strong possibility for life after
death. There are anecdotal accounts from thousands of people who
have clinically died and returned to life. But in my experience, only
about half of the people I encounter (outside of my client base) truly
believe that I am communicating with the dead.

"For those who believe, no explanation is necessary. For those who
do not believe, no explanation will suffice." That's a quote from Joseph
Dunninger, who was one of the most famous mentalists of all time.
Mentalists like Dunninger believe that psychics and mediums are not
accessing any subtle information at all, but are very skillfully tuning in
to body language, verbal cues, and other signs to read a person.

If you are convinced spirit people don't exist, and that you won't
exist after death, I won't make any attempts to change your mind. The
truth is, none of us knows, not with the kind of absolute certainty

the rational mind requires. If you believe, or are open to believing, I think you're in for a wonderful experience not only when you visit a medium, but when you begin to practice on your own. I've seen enough evidence through my own work to convince me that the spirit people are real. I'm more than happy to share my stories, but if someone challenges me on the possibility of spirit communication, I leave them to their own beliefs. More than one person has said to me, "How can you claim to talk to dead people?" My response is always the same. "They talk to me. What am I supposed to do, ignore them?"

Besides being a medium who works with the spirit people every day, I'm a person of great faith in God. My upbringing as a Catholic and training in a seminary taught me the beauty of resting in God's promise to bring me into His heaven when my physical life is over. I know I'll be in His presence, and reunited with my loved ones, too. I have faith and the benefit of personal evidence that life continues, so I'm always surprised by those who have the faith, but have no interest in the possible evidence.

I had lunch with an acquaintance not too long ago, and we were discussing my work. She is very devout, and gently informed me that mediumship was not acceptable to the Christian church. This wonderful lady didn't know that I knew she'd lost a child, and I wanted to grab her hands and say, "Don't you want to hear from her, in a way that would entirely convince you that she's still alive? Don't you want to know for sure that she is really all right, and still participating in the family?" As a lay minister, my acquaintance has great faith and a capacity for believing in the mysterious ways God works, and that is enormously comforting to her. Yet, in a way, it seems like turning down an opportunity to hear from a deceased loved one is like turning down modern medicine, because you'd rather rely on faith healing. But that's her choice, and I would never force my beliefs on her.

Belief in the afterlife is a deeply personal choice. Life after death can be neither proven nor disproved, so we must each decide individually whether we believe in the existence of spirit people. Don't ever feel the need to defend your belief or to convert another person to your viewpoint. I have a ready response for those who challenge me. I simply shrug my shoulders and say, "This is what I believe." Nobody can argue with that!

If They Are Around, How Do They Contact Us?

I find that the spirit people take every opportunity they can to let us know they're still around. I was once stretching on a mat at the gym, feeling both mentally and physically relaxed, when I felt a kind of tug to open my eyes and look up. Directly in front of me a woman was exercising on a stair-climber, and standing nearby was the spirit of her mother, who'd passed from breast cancer. I didn't feel comfortable going up to a stranger with headphones on and initiating a conversation about her dead mother, so I asked the spirit person to call her daughter's attention to mediumship in some other way. Whether she did or not I don't know.

Spirits take opportunities not only through professional mediums, but through anyone receptive to their presence. I received an e-mail from a client whose father I'd brought through in an earlier reading:

"I just wanted to let you know you were right. I, too, can communicate with [my dad]. Today he gave me and my family a huge sign. I bought chimes after his birthday, and they never rang or moved like I so desperately hoped. Then, this morning, the chimes were all tangled, and I knew immediately it was him. Hours later, after the kids got a chance to see, I yelled "Daddy, fix my chimes." Later that night my son said "Mommy, go look at the chimes," and they were perfectly normal again. My kids were in awe, we all told him we loved him and thanked him, then my son said "Grandpa, tangle them up again." I did not think it would happen, but fifteen minutes later my son called me, and the chimes were once again tangled, only this time perfectly criss-crossed like x's. Like someone delicately had to place them like that. There was no wind, no doors opening. We asked him to do something, and he did. It was a huge sign. Even my husband was in shock. There was no logical explanation for this at all. I needed to reach out to you, as you were the one who made me understand that we all have this ability, we just need to pay attention."

I do believe everyone can be contacted by loved ones in spirit. They'll contact us in any way that will make us believers. We simply need to be open to the experience. I find it also helps to acknowledge when our requests for contact have been answered. As in the example above, my client joyfully recognized her father's hand in the tangling and untangling of her wind chimes.

Another one of my clients knows her grandmother is answering her requests for help, because she finds a button within hours after sending a prayer to her. Another friend becomes aware of her mother's presence when she smells the perfume her mother always wore.

Our loved ones want more than anything to let us know that they're okay, they're still existing, and they're still loving us. If we're open to listening, they seem more than willing to talk.

CHAPTER 6

How Can You Tell If A Medium Is Ethical?

Here's another quote from The Amazing Dunninger: "There is one primary rule in the fakery of spirit mediumship. That is to concentrate upon persons who have suffered a bereavement."

I can't imagine the self-serving gall needed to take advantage of someone who is grieving the loss of a loved on. Because mediumship is such an edgy topic to begin with, I've set up a couple of ground rules to protect myself and my clients. For all of us in this profession, I am careful to avoid even the appearance of impropriety. Aside from the legal disclaimer that what I do is "for entertainment only," I adhere to a code of ethics that absolutely forbids the giving of advice. In addition, I will not see someone whose loved one went out in the previous six months. I tell potential clients that those who have passed away within the previous half-year are not available to me. It doesn't mean they are not safe in heaven, simply that I cannot reach them.

Recently deceased spirits will peek through anyway. They must know that my guest can handle their presence. But as a rule, I let my clients know that some time must pass before they will be connected to their loved one through me, anyway.

It still shocks me that there are charlatans and fakers out there, and what really irritates me is that they give the rest of us a bad name. I do everything I can to make sure my clients are receiving genuine spirit communication, from forgetting them if I've previously read them, to closing my eyes during a reading so I can't cold read them. If I have a repeat client, and a spirit person returns for them, I ask that they come through with totally new evidence or new details. I want every client to be certain that I'm not working from my memory, but only relaying impressions from the spirit.

A few years ago, I heard great things about a medium through an acquaintance. She praised his remarkable abilities and physical mediumship talents. The first time I went to see him I was prepared for a terrific show. About twenty of us gathered in his client's basement. No one was allowed to tape or take notes, which should have been a red flag right there. All the lights were extinguished, and the seams around the windows and were doors taped so we sat in total darkness. The medium, whom I'll call Hal, brought a trumpet, which is a cone made of tin or cardboard through which the spirits supposedly produce objects from their world.

The session began, and I eagerly awaited my reading. It was pitch black, and I couldn't see a thing except the glow-in-the dark tape on the edges of the trumpet, which seemed to be moving around randomly. He got to me and told me about the spirit guides he saw around me, Dr. Byrd and Little Moccasin, and conveyed a message that they would help me make a big decision. And then he moved on, leaving me unsatisfied and rather disappointed. I remember asking myself, "Who are these guides? Why have I never met them? What big decision?"

I left that evening with the funny feeling that I'd been had, but everyone around me was chattering with excitement about Hal's incredible talents. I began to second guess my instinct about what I'd witnessed.

If you can believe it, about a year later I went to see this guy again with a friend of mine. At this event, Hal passed out slips of paper and asked us to write down who we wished to hear from, while his assistant put blank index cards in a woven basket. Hal claimed he would pick up each of our slips of paper while blindfolded, and bring through the spirits we'd asked for. At the end of the event he would open up the basket and distribute art that the spirits made while they were communicating through him. The room was buzzing with happy expectation.

I wasn't specifically looking for a hoax to unfold, but there signs right from the beginning. First, Hal insisted we legibly print the first names of our loved ones in spirit. Then he put cotton pads over his eyes and taped them shut, but in such a way that it was clear he could see if he looked straight down. He covered and sealed the woven basked with the blank index cards inside, and began to pick up our papers. I noticed that even though he was supposedly blindfolded, he was turning all the papers so they faced the same way—with the writing up. Hal suddenly remembered he hadn't put the markers in the art basket, so he handed the covered basket to his assistant, who left the room with it. When he returned, he claimed he had sealed the markers inside with the blank index cards. The reading began, and I could plainly see Hal tilt his head back ever so slightly and move each slip of paper very close to his body in order read it. I looked around in disbelief, but no one except my friend seemed to notice.

Soon after he began, Hal announced that the spirits of Stanley and William were with him. We all looked around at each other, waiting for someone to claim these two spirits. Hal repeated himself, and suddenly I realized he was reading *my* paper. I didn't recognize the names, because Stanley was my Polish grandfather, whom we called *Dziadzie,* and William was my Dad, whom we called *Jefe.* I said they belonged to me, and was told—again, if you can believe it—that they were here to help me make a big decision. He didn't identify either one by their relationship to me, or give me any kind of personal message. He simply moved on to the next paper.

When he was done, I was given my spirit art card from the basket. It had the names once again of guides I'd never heard of printed on the back, and a black and white photograph of a person on the front, covered all over with crayon and marker. I was so disgusted at this point, my friend and I made our excuses to avoid the coffee hour afterwards. We weren't getting away that easily, however. Hal's assistant insisted on scanning the fronts and backs of our cards before we left. I suspect the reason for that was in case we every came back, Hal would need to produce the same guides. The minute we got home, we scraped off the crayon and found that the pictures were from old catalogs and advertisements, which had been photocopied on to the index cards. I'd foolishly paid $150 and driven two hours for that event!

I saw recently that Hal will be appearing at a regional New Age shop with his spirit readings again, and it makes me so angry to know that he is taking advantage of hopeful people. Spirit communication *is* real. I've seen it and experienced it myself. This so-called medium could do the real thing if he applied himself to learning how, instead of faking his way to the bank.

What I did learn from Hal is that I should have paid attention to my own instincts about him, instead of letting myself be convinced by the crowd and the showmanship.

The best way to connect with a trustworthy medium is by referral from someone you trust. The medium should charge a reasonable fee that reflects time spent with him or her, and whether you're having a private reading or being read as part of a group. If you're going to be in a group or audience, find out the size of the crowd and also ask whether you're guaranteed a reading. When I do the spirit communication portion of the service at a nearby Spiritualist Church, I have only about twenty minutes and can't guarantee everyone in the congregation a reading. When I do open or private circles I limit the number of guests so that I can guarantee everyone gets a message from a spirit person *they can identify.* A medium should always connect you with at least one spirit you can concretely validate. It's one thing to have a medium share their impressions about spirit guides around you, but if that's all that's coming through for you, find another practitioner.

Don't go by fame alone, either. I once went up to Lilydale, which is arguably the medium capital of the United States. I paid $80 for a half-hour reading with one of the most famous mediums there, and it was disappointing to say the least. The guy looked so bored to be reading yet another tourist, and he gave me entirely generic information. He seemed to cold read me, and then gave me advice based on the questions he'd asked me before and during the session. (To be fair, a friend had a reading from him also and was pleased that the medium brought in the family dog).

If the medium cannot connect you with a spirit for one reason or another, they should be able to discern that shortly after beginning the session. An ethical medium will tell you so, and will return your money if you've paid in advance. I was unable to bring in spirit people only once, and it happened during a message circle at a healing arts center. There was a guest seated directly across the table from me, and I could see a crowd of spirit people around her, all eager to express gratitude. Nevertheless, not one single spirit was significant or recognizable to her. The spirit people were incredibly specific, too. One woman had died during her eighth month of pregnancy. One man spent his last years bent almost double in a wheelchair, due to a degenerative disease of the spine, and had perished from a respiratory infection. Dozens more came through, yet none of these wonderful spirits could be identified by my guest. We were both getting frustrated as time wore on, and all the other guests had been read. I finally closed the circle and offered to return the fee to guest I couldn't read. She didn't take her money back, but as she was walking out the door she said, "I work in a hospital emergency room, and all of those people you described were people who passed through here, but I didn't know them."

Aha! Suddenly it all made sense. I pulled her back in for a moment and shared with her the message every single one of those lovely spirit people had come through to say: "Thank you! You made my passing easier. I saw you with my family when they got the news. Thank you!"

This wonderful guest was moved to tears knowing how she had impacted so many people with her work. And if I get a whole bunch of spirit folk my guest can't identify, I've learned to ask "Do you work in a hospital?"

Get a referral, ask questions about how the medium works, be sure you understand the price and the process, and speak up right away if you don't feel the session is going well. An ethical medium wants to satisfy both her physical clients and her spirit clients, and values her reputation.

Above all, trust your own instincts. It is against the law for any psychic medium to ask for money to remove a curse, or to claim that some sort of doom awaits you unless you return with more money or for more sessions. It is unethical for a psychic medium to suggest that illness or death is in your near future, or that bad spirits are attached to you. If it feels like you're being scammed, you probably are.

CHAPTER 7

Isn't It Just Mind Reading?

Someone once asked me if I'm really receiving communication from spirit people, or if I'm just reading a client's mind. Am I somehow picking up on who the client really wants to hear from, and reflecting back the details that they're thinking about? It's a valid question, and one I've often wondered about myself. Over the years I've come to feel quite satisfied that it is indeed spirit people, due to a number of factors.

First, spirits often come through whom clients aren't expecting to hear from, or whom they hadn't thought about in years. At recent reading, the young man who was one of my guests had trouble placing the spirit at first.

As I tuned in, I said to him, "Someone is coming through and showing me... an... um... really? Do I have to say this?" I began laughing out loud, and I knew I was blushing. I had to say what I was being shown, which was a huge erection. I finally managed to share what I was seeing, and said "When a spirit person shows me this it means he was really, really manly, a man's man, or very masculine, or had a lot of girlfriends, or was really into sex. He shows me also beneath it, in what we would call the 'down there' area, that something was wrong. Do you know who I'm talking about?"

"I have no idea, that's really weird," said my guest.

"This is a man who was kind of a blue collar guy, who would have bragged about this. He shows me having been in the service, he served and came back, not someone who died in the service. And I feel that he kept the military haircut. He gives me the feeling of being fifty-ish."

After a long pause, the young man said "I know someone like that, but I don't know where he is or if he's dead."

"Does this sound like him?"

"Yes."

"Then he's dead," I said with as much humor as the spirit man was giving me.

"He took too much viagra one day, he was a real comedian. He was about fifty. He was hanging out with prostitutes all night, and he had to go to the hospital because his erection wouldn't go away."

"Well, I'm here to tell you he's dead. *He's* here to tell you he's dead, and experiencing this whacky sort of joy, still carrying on as a comedian. He comes through to say 'Hi.' Do you know a Frances or a Frank?"

"His name is Frank, that's his name."

Frank went on to give a message to my guest, which had everyone laughing. I couldn't have been reading my guest's mind in this case, as he hadn't thought about Frank in years, nor was he aware of his passing.

At another circle some time ago, a child came through, showing himself in a car seat and claiming to have passed in an accident. I kept wanting to give this child to a certain guest in the circle, but she couldn't identify him. Without connecting him to anyone, I carried on with other messages, but he was always there on the fringe. Finally, towards the end of the evening, the woman I kept trying to come to with the baby called out that she knew who he was (the details appear later in this book). My guest didn't come to the circle expecting to hear from anyone outside her immediate circle, but this little spirit saw an opportunity to get a message through. If she wasn't expecting to hear from this child, I couldn't have read her mind.

Second, clients sometimes come in hoping to hear from a particular person in spirit, and instead get messages from several others. Because of the way I structure my sessions, I don't allow clients to tell me who they're hoping to hear from before the reading. I don't want any advance knowledge about loved ones who have passed away. If I were really just mind reading, wouldn't I pick up on the one person my guest really wanted to hear from?

A third reason I believe I'm not mind reading, but communicating with spirit can be found in Chapter Four, where I describe how Lorraine's mother came through to tell her about an upcoming pregnancy by artificial insemination. Lorraine couldn't imagine who her mother was talking about, so there is no way she could have had this information in her mind for me to read. Below is another example of the spirit knowing what the client does not.

A young lady and her boyfriend came for a private reading. Both of their brothers had passed away many years apart, yet they both came through raising a toast to the couple in front of me. It seemed that the brothers were definitely toasting them both, so I inquired if they were engaged to be married. The answer was no. The spirit brothers kept toasting however, so I told the couple that they could expect an engagement or pregnancy. They protested loudly and laughingly, yet several weeks later I received this e-mail:

"Hey Priscilla, I just want to say thank you... you truly have an amazing gift... I saw you in January with my boyfriend. When we sat down you said our brothers where there and then you said they keep saying congratulations... turns out I'm eight weeks pregnant [and] we are engaged..."

I receive multiple after-the-fact validations like this, which seem to come as a direct message from the spirit people. I don't believe I'd be able to pass on these messages if I were simply mind reading.

Another reason I believe what transpires is more than mind reading, involves items or spirits the client can't identify or remember during our reading, but which are actually found to be true after talking to a friend or family member. One spirit person named Rusty had a message for his wife, who was the friend of a guest. He kept talking about a huge frozen drink, which my guest could not identify. After sharing this message with her friend, I received this e-mail from her:

"After [the] message circle this evening, I called Rusty's wife; she recalls a frozen margarita so large they had to stand on a chair to drink it and shared it with two straws!!"

Sometimes my guests only get as far as the driveway before running back with validation. Others call on the way home after speaking to a family member. One young woman called to tell me "you asked me if the older gentleman, whom I believed to be my grandfather, had ever been in the military. You were correct. My mother confirmed it."

If this weren't coming from a spirit person, how could I know it?

If my guest herself didn't know, how could I read her mind and reflect her own knowledge back to her?

Finally, I'm convinced it's more than mind reading, because mediumship just feels so different from psychic readings, when I am tuning into a client's mind. Psychic readings and spirit communications each have a unique quality to them. Simply tuning into the sixth sense for a psychic reading, I'm not bumping into any spirits before the appointment. Before a mediumship session, I feel that crazy energy on my porch, like the spirit people are getting ready for our appointment, too. If I were just mind reading, I wouldn't sense the presence of spirit people in advance, nor would I sense their departure if the appointment is cancelled.

I remember a spirit communication appointment I'd scheduled for 7:00 p.m. one evening. As usual, I called the day before to confirm the appointment. My client concurred that we would meet as scheduled, but all throughout the day of the appointment I kept feeling as though I should call her to re-confirm. There was absolutely no spirit activity in my house. Not wanting to appear neurotic, I decided to forego a double-check. Nevertheless, I couldn't understand why my porch felt so empty. So it really came as no surprise when my client didn't show. I called her at 7:20 p.m., and when she answered the phone she was completely surprised that she wasn't where she promised to be. Even though we'd spoken the day before, she was distracted during that confirmation call, and thought our appointment was for the following night. Her spirit people had indeed communicated to me—by not showing up—that she wasn't going to show up either.

One winter night in February, I was preparing to head out for a regular monthly message circle in a nearby town. I was buzzing with energy as I looked forward to meeting the spirit people who'd been gathering in my house all day long. Backing out of my driveway however, my car slid firmly into a snow bank, and stuck there. Still hoping I could shovel my way out, I went into the house to call the venue where I was scheduled to appear.

The moment I walked into my house I felt the complete absence of the spirit people. There was no energy, they were entirely gone. I knew in an instant I wouldn't be meeting the guests at the circle, nor bringing through their spirit people. I did call the venue then, not to tell them I'd be late, as I'd hoped, but to cancel the event. And while I did spend about an hour trying to dig out my car, I wasn't surprised that I didn't succeed, and that the evening didn't go as planned. The spirit people had already informed me.

Spirit people give me a distinct sense of their presence, which is a palpable energy around me and my house. They communicate their absence too, when I feel that energy disappear. That feels an awful lot like interaction with spirit people, and not mind reading.

There may be evidence supporting the other conclusion, too. Some of my clients ask in advance for a certain spirit to come through. They tell me they've meditated or prayed, or simply wished really hard that their loved one would appear. More than one client has told me that they set up a little test, asking their loved one in spirit to mention a special event or detail. I suppose it's possible in those instances for a medium to be reading the client's mind rather than communicating with their spirit person.

For example, during a private reading for a woman and her friend, I became aware of a young man.

"He comes in and he is a peer, like a brother or cousin. He shows me a microphone, like he is singing into a microphone or making an announcement."

"I'm not sure who that is. There isn't anyone in my family who used a microphone," said my client.

"He shows me that he's kind of joking, like maybe he's singing karaoke. Does that make sense? Did you just go to a karaoke bar?" I asked. The spirit man was amplifying this impression.

"No, I don't know what that means," she answered.

I asked him to clarify, because he wasn't moving on past the microphone. I begged him for other details, but again he zeroed in on the microphone he was holding, giving me a real close up view. And then I saw it.

"Wait, it's not a microphone he's holding," I said, "it's a hairbrush! He's fooling around, singing into a hairbrush like it's a microphone."

"Oh my God, that's my brother!" she shouted. "I thought it was him but I couldn't be sure. Right when you said that, I remembered telling him before he died if he ever came to me, he would have to show me that so I could believe it was really him!"

She was laughing and crying at the same time, in total disbelief. I felt satisfied that I made this connection because as soon as she acknowledged him, I felt that crazy *zing!* up my spine. That funny energy always accompanies a spirit's joy when he's been recognized. Could an argument be made that I tapped into some long-buried deal she made with her brother, that even she herself had forgotten? It's certainly possible.

I went on to deliver the brother's message to her, which I didn't understand, but which was completely relevant for my client. I don't believe I could read a message in someone's mind, when I don't myself understand it. So, in the end, I still feel that mediumship is truly spirit communication, and not just mind reading.

I had a tough time reading a particular guest one night. The circle took place at a healing arts facility where I hold regular events, and this guest was one of the partners in the business. She had never been to one of my circles before, and I was eager to impress her. I started to sweat a little as the evening wore on, because plenty of spirits were coming through for the rest of the guests, but Betty was a big blank.

Finally, I asked all the other spirit people to step back for just a moment so I could focus on Betty's energy. I became aware, very vaguely, of a male who had a romantic attachment to her. Betty could only give a vague validation, because whatever I could sense was rather generic. Then, to my surprise, this figure held a puppy out to me. Recognizing the hint he'd thrown me, I said "He's holding a puppy, he says tell her about the puppy!" I was probably more excited than Betty, because I finally got a specific detail. She quietly acknowledged it was her ex-husband, and that she'd had a feeling he would show up; she had said to him "If it's really you, come in with the puppy."

This was clearly a wish set forth by the guest, so was I accessing her thoughts or was I really communicating with her husband? I don't know the answer for certain, and probably never will until I go out myself. Whether it's mind reading or spirit communication is something each person will have to decide for himself. Either way, the end result is still pretty cool, isn't it?

CHAPTER 8

What About Evil Spirits?

I personally don't believe in evil, nor do I allow any reference to it during my readings or circles. Many people don't agree, and some of them are quite learned spiritual leaders in both traditional and New Age belief systems. A Christian pastor I know quite fervently disagrees with me. She's spent many years performing exorcisms, and claims to have encountered evil in different forms. Some of the most celebrated psychic mediums practicing today describe dark forces or evil entities. They talk about "lost souls" and those who don't know that they're dead. One famous medium wrote a whole chapter in a best-selling book on where suicides go when they die, which, according to him, was not heaven but some hazy level between earth and hell.

No one can tell us what heaven or hell is like, no matter how many spirit communications they've facilitated. Remember, the spirit people have to impress their thoughts and feelings on *our minds,* using our experience, history, vocabulary, and the various symbols that have meaning for us. So, if a male in spirit only spoke Portuguese when he was alive, for example, he isn't going to speak to me in Portuguese during a reading, because I don't understand that language. Instead, he'll show me a map of Portugal, or the flag, or will give me the taste of Madeira wine, so that I can say to my guests, "There is a man here in spirit who comes from Portugal." Once that spirit is acknowledged, then he'll impress me with his message. He does that is by stirring up something I can reference, somewhere in my own life experience, or by the use of a previous symbol I've established in other readings.

When a medium or psychic describes heaven to you, or tells you "this is what *really* happens after you die," please consider that a mortal human being is unlikely to know that with absolute certainty.

If my idea of heaven is a beautiful, wide open meadow with harp music swelling in the background, the spirit person who wants to say he's in heaven is going to show me that picture. Why? Because a symbol is a very efficient way of getting a message across. Does his heaven really look like that? Nobody knows. Perhaps heaven is what we expect it to be, or maybe it defies description. I won't know till I get there, and neither will any other medium or spiritual genius, no matter how confident they sound.

I came across a simple and profound saying years ago, which I've never forgotten (though I've forgotten who said it—my apologies): *There is no dark switch.*

This doesn't mean there's no darkness, just that it isn't itself a force, the way light is. When you bring light into a dark room with a switch, a candle, or a flashlight, the light is a force of its own that spreads out and dispels darkness. It's impossible to bring dark into a light-filled room, the way you can bring light into a dark-filled room.

I apply this concept to the good versus evil question. The way I see it, there is light (God) and varying degrees of distance from light (God). I also believe that it is only we humans who perceive distance from God. I think people keep forgetting that God isn't a human being, with an ego, old resentments, and memories of someone else's abuse, neglect, or abandonment. All of those emotions belong to human personalities. I don't mean to say they're not real, valid, or justified, only to say that God is probably above them, if we're to believe all that's written about Him.

If we could all remember or see how holy and perfect we are at this instant, we would know with one hundred percent certainty that we were children of God. And if I am a child of God, so must you be, too. If I recognize the Divinity in you, how could I ever cause you harm?

Are those people who commit heinous acts evil, as my pastor friend claims? I'm not so sure. Granted, neither I nor anyone I love has ever been the victim of a violent crime, and perhaps I'd feel differently if that weren't the case. But I do know, intellectually if not experientially, that if I see as God sees, and love as God loves, that everyone will be perfect and forgivable in my eyes, and those who commit terrible acts have actually just forgotten who they really are.

In his book *The Shack* by William P. Young, the narrator, who has lost a child to a pedophile, is begging God for help in forgiving his daughter's killer. At one point in the story, God says to him that he must choose to consign one of his other children to hell. The narrator admits that each of his other children can be challenging at times, but none are irredeemable. In total anguish he cries, "take me instead, don't send any of my children to hell!" And God points out that this is exactly what Jesus did; he begged his Father not to consign any of His children to hell and offered his own life up instead.

Whether or not you're a Christian, it's a poignant story. God loves all of His children unconditionally, so who are we humans to say a certain person will end up in hell, or will turn into a lost soul or an evil spirit?

A Course In Miracles holds that there is only love and fear, and only love is real. If only love—only God—is real, how can there be any force in opposition? The dual nature of the world we live in means there is day and night, good and bad, right and wrong. But once we go out to the spirit world I believe we leave behind the physical world, and all the accompanying judgments that go with it. We see finally that there is no separation, and if all are one and one with God, than there really is no dual nature after all.

These concepts can be very hard to integrate into our thinking. They run counter to the way we are raised, which emphasizes reliance on the intellectual, rational mind. The rational mind needs black and white in order to analyze and solve problems, to make decisions and judgments. I believe we are asked spiritually to abandon the need to make judgments, to see ourselves and God in everyone, and act accordingly. "Do unto others as you would have them do unto you" is called the Golden Rule for good reason.

The moment we frame a judgment or definition around something or someone, then whatever falls outside of that framework becomes its opposite. For instance, if I define myself as a "good" person because of all the things I do and believe, there are automatically going to be people who fall outside of that definition, and that logically makes them "other than good." A separation is born. If I can manage to suspend a definition of myself (intellectually) and carry on putting

God first throughout my day, I am just *being*. And if *I am*, and no more than that, I can live in the moment as one with the world and people around me.

St. Francis is said to have written, "Teach the Word of God wherever you go, and only when necessary use words." He is suggesting that we simply recognize who we are and *be*, and that others will follow our example. St. Francis is also credited with a prayer urging us to give away that which we most need, because "it is only in giving that we receive." What a succinct and poetic way to remind us that we are all one child of God.

Once during a healing session I was receiving from a colleague, I entered a very blissful trance state. As part of his practice, the healer whispered to me, "Who are you?" and my immediate internal response was "I am God's thought of Himself." Not my words, and words that certainly felt truer than any I could have come up with myself. I came out of that healing session with a brand new appreciation for my fellow human beings. After all, if I'm God's thought of Himself, so must be every person I encounter, from the grouchy toll-taker to the hardened criminal.

If we're all part of God, how is it possible some of us will go to eternal fire and others will be lifted up? Or, how is it possible, as some mediums have written, that we go to different levels of heaven? I don't believe God loves us in different degrees, so I don't believe we have to earn our way up the heavenly ladder. God already loves us; God already sees our perfection. The spirit people themselves taught me that unbaptized babies, criminals, suicides, and saints all end up in the same heaven. We may have work to do there, we may choose to return to earth in physical form to try again, but when we go out, I believe we all fall into God's welcoming embrace no matter what kind of life we've led.

I believe those people classified as evil have lost their way. Perhaps they are so far from love they wouldn't recognize it if it walked up and kissed them on the cheek. The God I believe in wouldn't punish them for what they lost, but would show them where to find it.

As for evil spirits, I don't believe in their existence either. If there aren't truly evil people, how can there be evil spirits? Historically it made sense to believe in evil. Simple people needed explanations for terrible things that happened in the world, and the religious institutions needed a way to control the population. Perhaps the time has come now to focus on how wonderful we are as human people, rather than judge ourselves or others.

I'm not claiming to be an authority on the subject by any means. I can only share with you the beliefs I've crafted after years of study and personal experience working with the spirit people. I am always willing to be shown a better way. I have been wrong before and I may be wrong about evil. In fact, my pastor friend said I would never know when evil hooked me, because once it did, my moral compass would be so far out of whack I'd be unable to judge for myself. For now, I'm confident that the work I do brings hope and closure to living people, and excitement and opportunity to the spirit people, who continue to tell me this will all make sense when we, too, are dead. The spirit people tell me, and I believe them, that judgment doesn't start at physical death, it stops there.

PART THREE

Spirit People & Their World

CHAPTER 9

Where Are They?

Only on a few occasions have the spirit people talked to be me about their environment. It seems to be of little importance in a reading or message circle. They have shown me, by showing my clients, that they are with family members or friends, and quite often with companion animals. While they haven't detailed the spirit world to me, they have illustrated their visits to the physical world.

During a private reading with a young woman, I asked her husband in spirit about his whereabouts. He described something quite poetic. He said he looked for the "likes" in his wife's energy field. He would identify the place where she held the memory or the energy of the things she liked, and he would "hang out there." He said, "When I can find the part where you liked me, I will go there." He showed me that, to him, those parts looked something like the burnished spots on a bronze sculpture, or like the way light streams through an old fashioned perforated tin lantern. He said that he slipped right into those "likes" and was suspended there, as though he were relaxing in a hammock.

My guest left after shedding a few joyful tears, knowing that all she had to do was recall her feelings of admiration, friendship, and love for her husband, and he would be as close to her as if he had his arms around her.

At a private message circle for a family matriarch, her six daughters, and two granddaughters, I kept hearing from a male spirit that none present could identify. He had been showing me a lion, which I took as a symbol for a name, such as Leo or Leon. The name didn't connect with anyone. As often happens, the unidentified spirit person (I call them U.S.P.'s) will stay around the circle while other spirit people come in, occasionally stepping forward to add another detail about their identity, until they can be validated. As I was getting ready to close, I felt the presence of this spirit man press forward one more time. I was about to announce him once again when one of the guests asked if she could ask a question.

"Of course!" I replied

"Could you bring in a spirit if I tell you his name?" She told me her brother-in-law's name, and I felt the *zing!* up my spine right away.

"He's here already, he's been here the whole time." I described the spirit man once again, but my guest didn't look convinced.

"Can you tell me something more about him?"

The spirit man showed me the lion once again, but really seemed to press it into me, as though he were saying, *try harder.* Suddenly I knew what the spirit had been impressing upon me.

"He's in Africa," I said, "he travels there frequently. I get the sense now that he watches over someone there, or he has business there."

This got a very satisfied reaction from my guests, as they described a cousin who travels frequently to Africa on business. All the ladies in the circle were delighted to know that this brother-in-law was watching over another family member while he was far from home.

Spirit people tell me that they travel with family members, attend weddings and baptisms, and generally still participate in family life even though they have passed away. I'm no closer to an understanding of the spirit world than when I began my career, but I am confident that our loved ones frequently check in with the physical world.

What Do They Do There, Anyway?

Some spirit people refer to themselves as being "very busy." On more than one occasion, when a repeat client calls yet again on a loved one, that spirit has expressed something a little like impatience. As though they are saying, "*What?* I'm busy!" Sometimes during a message circle, a spirit will pop in for only a moment, as though they're passing through. They indicate to me that they have to get back to what they're doing, though what that is I've never been told.

I've noticed that there doesn't appear to be time in the spirit world. Here on planet earth we are encouraged to be industrious and to use our time wisely, to be efficient and productive. These are all qualities that are founded in religious beliefs or cultural beliefs, and are not necessarily one of the qualities of just *being*. I don't get the sense that the spirit people are punching a clock, or counting the hours, or measuring their lives out in a framework of time passing. When they refer to being busy, or having to go, I sense they are not so much in a hurry, but rather perhaps have limited energy or ability to continue dumping impressions into my sixth sense.

They have a funny sense of their time here in the physical world, too. Those who lived into their golden years describe themselves as passing away "towards the end of my life." I love that expression! Those who cross over at an early age often say "I passed before my time."

Spirit people who have had a hand in their own early passing frequently inform me that they are still maturing, and will continue to do so until they achieve the "prime of their life." If a young person commits suicide, his spirit tells us he continues to work on the challenges he couldn't face here, with guidance and support from other spirit people. He is able to advance and mature through those challenges in the spirit world. Knowing that a life wasn't simply cut short brings much relief to the families of such spirits.

During one circle a guest's mother came through first, and, after we identified her, continued to hang around. My guest asked if her mother had a particular message for her, but the spirit mother simply continued to remind me that she was there. Finally, at the end of our circle, she came through with her message, which she conveyed through the tale of St. Christopher.

For those of you who don't know, the story of St. Christopher begins when a traveler approaches a fast-moving river. He notices a small child on the bank who asks to be carried across. The traveler (Christopher) agrees and puts the child on his shoulders. As he fords the river, the baby gets heavier and heavier, until Christopher is leaning on his staff and staggering through the dangerous water, risking his own life. When he finally reaches the other side, he puts the child down and says, essentially, "What the heck just happened!?"

The child says he is Jesus, and he is so heavy because he carries the weight of all the sin in the world. Christopher is canonized and becomes the Patron Saint of Travelers. He is de-canonized a century or so later.

After the spirit mother had me tell this story, she impressed on me that she herself had carried a terrible sin, or so she'd thought. She hid this sin, and judged herself very harshly all through her life. When she finally went out, she learned that what she had carried had no weight in the spirit world. It was her *own* judgment, not God's, that made that burden so heavy. All that wasted energy! She told us to drop our harsh self-judgments, and to learn to forgive ourselves.

She told us all that she had taken on some sort of teaching or preaching work in the spirit world. It was her job to get the word out that God will never judge us as harshly as we judge ourselves.

I distinctly remember another busy spirit during a message circle. The evening was winding down, and I was getting ready to close. A family of three women asked if I would bring someone through for them, who hadn't come in. I don't often follow through with such a request, because that lends itself more to a private reading. Furthermore, if the spirit person hasn't come through on his own, I believe he's engaged in something much more important.

It was still early, so I decided to comply with their request. I asked for their loved one's first name, and went looking. What that means is, I close my eyes (I'm visual, and this helps me concentrate), and, instead of waiting for something to appear on the inside of my eyelids, I push out into the darkness that I see there. I stretch my vision as if I'm peering towards a very far off horizon, to see if I can detect any movement there, or any change. I may do that looking left, center, and right. I try to be patient, all while my conscious mind is taunting me: *"Oh boy, you're coming up short. These poor people can see right through you. They can see you don't know what you're doing. They can see you're a fraud."* (Yes, that stuff goes through my mind every now and then. I don't usually believe it, but when I have to look, summon, or fight for an impression, I begin to doubt myself. The clock is ticking, everyone's waiting, and I'm already ready to turn off the "Open For Business" sign and go home).

I also tune in to my feelings. I concentrate hard on locating or identifying any twinge or emotion that even faintly crops up. My feeling is, if a spirit person didn't show up at a circle, either he has a very good reason for staying away, or I am not picking up on his frequency. So in this exercise I just heighten my awareness as much as I can. It's difficult to describe, and rather difficult to do. I can't sustain it for more than a few seconds. It's like diving into a pool to retrieve something from the bottom of the deep end. I can only dive down for a few seconds before coming back up for air. And every time I have to come back up, I'm aware that people are waiting for me to deliver. It's pretty stressful, which is the perfect way *not* to feel when trying to find a spirit person.

Finally, after a couple of minutes of this kind of work, I thought I felt something. I leapt on it like a terrier, and began to drag it back from the far horizon. By that I mean that I pour all of my concentration on that feeling, until I can make sense of it with my conscious mind.

I'd gotten a very slight feeling of being out of balance. I brought it up to the family, with my usual connection of recreational or pharmaceutical drug use. They confirmed pharmaceutical drug use. We got a little closer to identifying him clearly when I saw him stick out his tongue at me, and it was evident he was making fun of me. The spirit man continued to offer details about heart-break, smoking, alcohol, and depression.

"Was he in general an impatient person?" I asked the family, because he kept giving me the feeling of "Enough! I'm very busy! Wrap it up!"

"What does he say?" the mother asked.

"He says 'they don't have their hooks in me any more,'" I answered, which caused quite a lot of laughter from the family. He died from complications of alcoholism, after a lengthy stay in the hospital, hooked up to things. He talked about a richness or texture in his perception now that he wasn't able to enjoy before, which seemed to describe emerging from the fog of alcoholism.

The family wanted to keep their loved one here, but he was very impatient. If you've ever had to get away from a conversation or get off the phone because you're in a rush and have a lot to do—and the other person keeps talking—you'll understand the impression the

spirit was giving me. He had to go, he was backing up, he had no
time to answer these questions, because he had to get back to what
he was doing. I begged this impatient spirit for one more detail, one
really specific message that would comfort his people.

"He's talking about Edgar Allen Poe, and his poem about the Raven,
specifically the line about knocking at the chamber door. He said this
knocking would be how you know him when he comes to visit."

One family member gave a happy shout, "I hear knocking on the
door all the time and there's never anyone there! I always felt it was him!"

With this solid validation the spirit person seemed to pack up his
energy really quickly and rush off. I wanted to ask him where he was
going and what he was doing that he had to get back to. I wanted to
know why he hadn't voluntarily shown up during the circle. But even
before I got those thoughts formulated he told me, "Not now!" and left.

My personal conclusion is that the spirit people are occupied
somehow, either in helping people cross over, working out judgment
issues, or in some endeavor that is entirely beyond my understanding,
but which clearly is important to them.

Do They Still Have Feelings?

Some of the most poignant messages to come through in readings
center around forgiveness or apologies. I can't count the number of
spirit mothers and fathers who come through acknowledging that
they could have been better parents.

A certain woman comes to see me every so often just to hear from
her father in spirit. The first time she came for a reading, he came
through calling her "Princess," which brought instant tears to her eyes.

I sensed almost immediately that he hadn't called her "Princess" in
a very long time. As she had grown up, he'd struggled with personal
disappointments and a stalled career, and had projected his frustration
onto her. When he came through, he did so with such tenderness that
it nearly brought tears to my eyes, too. He acknowledged that he was
too wrapped up in his own sense of failure to notice her achievements.
She tearfully validated this, and continued nodding her head when I
passed on his message that he saw now how hard she had been trying
to win his approval. He told her that even though he wasn't able to say

how proud he was of her while he was alive, he promised he would tell her now, every single time she needed to hear it.

That was about four years ago, and when she returns for a reading and I connect with her father, he proudly mentions all of her accomplishments. He'd seen her start her own business, congratulated her on the birth of his first grandchild, and even gave her fatherly advice. She leaves feeling satisfied that her father does indeed see and acknowledge her accomplishments, and that she truly does have his affection and approval.

Another client who has been a regular for many years, came recently for a reading. In all the time I've been reading for her, her father in spirit has never come through. Because I'd gotten to know her as time passed, I knew from her stories that her father was a terrible alcoholic, a mean drunk, who would come home from a night out and terrorize her mother and herself. The stories of how she had to hide from him as a small child were heartbreaking. When he passed away she felt nothing but relief.

At our most recent reading, I felt the presence of a man in spirit that I hadn't met before. He gave me his initial, W, and a few other details. My client acknowledged that it might be her father, though I was reluctant to agree with her. I didn't feel, through clairsentience, that I was drunk. As a clairsentient, I translate the feelings the spirit person gives to me, and whenever I've dealt with alcoholics or drug addicts or even those on heavy doses of prescription medication, I've felt dizzy, confused, or drugged. None of those clairsentient feelings came through, so I continued on.

"He shows me a target, like one would use for darts or archery. He shows me that he has a gun, and that he almost drowned."

"I did shoot a bow and arrow with my father in the backyard, he really enjoyed doing that. And he did almost drown while he was in the navy. I think that's him, though the gun doesn't make any sense."

I asked the spirit person for something that would clarify, once and for all, that this was the mean drunk father I'd heard about.

"He shows me a gun, but it looks like a cartoon shotgun, like Elmer Fudd would carry. It's a gun, but it's also a cartoon gun. Does this make sense?"

My client's eyes widened and a big smile appeared on her face. She told me the story of how, at four years old, she'd been watching a Bugs Bunny cartoon. One of the characters kept shooting another one over and over, turning into a puff of smoke and then reappearing. Thinking that looked like fun, she had gone upstairs and dug her father's handgun out of the night stand. She put the barrel to her temple, and remembers thinking, "this is really heavy." She was about to pull the trigger when her mother walked in and prevented a real catastrophe. We clearly were hearing from her father in spirit.

I asked him why he didn't come through with the drunk feeling. He told me I only knew that story about him, and his daughter knew I knew it, so it wouldn't be quite so authentic. "Besides," he said, "I'm not like that anymore." He continued to give a message to his daughter that he acknowledged his terrible actions, and left her with some of the few good and relief-filled moments of their time together.

An interesting thing I've noticed is that the spirit people don't really apologize, exactly. They will always acknowledge if they'd made bad decisions, or were unpleasant to be with, or didn't believe in an afterlife (that's my favorite). But very often their motive in doing so seems to be more as an identifying characteristic rather than an apology. While some of my physical guests would really love to hear an apology, there is something so beautifully poetic about a simple acknowledgment—it shows that the spirit people are totally unhooked from the human need to make a judgment.

I once asked a spirit to impress upon me how that was possible, because the world we live in is completely either/or, black/white, and us/them. It's so hard to escape this tendency to assign good or bad labels to an action or a person. He showed me something I'd seen before, even used before, in my former practice as a clinical hypnotist. On the screen of my mind's eye, I seemed to be watching a football game from the sidelines. I watched the players smash into each other, shove each other around aggressively, swear at each other, and sustain injuries. It was an ugly, too-close-for-comfort vision. But then I felt myself receding from the edge of the action, to much higher up, where I could see the whole field. From there it was much easier to see the purpose of that aggression. I could see that there was a goal and that there was actually an art to the game. From this vantage point, the spirit person showed me how what they see differs from what we experience here in our physical bodies. Once removed from physical life, the spirit people can see that their actions, even if unpleasant to those they encountered, were actually an essential part of a learning experience. They don't feel the need to say that they were a bad person, any more than someone watching a football game would say that a particularly aggressive player was bad person.

The language they impress on my sixth sense reflects this. For instance, someone who has overdosed on drugs will usually say, "I had a hand in my own passing." Those who have let bad habits lead to their death will usually say, "I made a series of bad decisions and let go control of my life." Even those who have knowingly taken actions that lead directly to their passing will say, "I took myself out very early."

At a message circle for a family in my home, a young man came through quite strongly right away. As a matter of fact, he was the only non-family member spirit to appear that evening. He gave me a sense of losing control, and of being very muddy in my thinking. I mentioned right away that he was showing me a death connected to drugs or alcohol. The tearful young woman to my right nodded her head.

"He gives me an 'M' name, like Matt or Matthew."

"Yes, that was his name."

"He is acknowledging a bad decision, but he gives me the feeling that he didn't usually make bad decisions, and that this one was really bad. It caused him to go out very early."

"He overdosed on heroin the first time he tried it," she said.

I began to feel an intense compassion from the spirit, as he went on to talk about someone else being there with him before he died.

"Matt tells me that someone is feeling very guilty about his passing, as though he should have done something to help him. This person, still here, is feeling tremendous guilt that Matt died."

Her tears made it such that my guest could only nod.

"Matt wants to say to this person that he himself is fully responsible for his bad decision, and that there was nothing anyone could have or should have done to stop him. He is acknowledging that his passing was entirely at his own hands, and no one should feel guilt about it. It was a bad decision that lead to serious consequences. He isn't being punished, and no one else should punish themselves about it either."

My guest was able to say that a mutual friend had seen Matt overdosing, and had run away without calling for help. He was in terrible emotional pain as a result of it.

"Matt shows me that he wants this friend to stop feeling guilt. He shows me as though he is taking two huge hooks out of him, like giant meat hooks of guilt out of his friend. Please pass on this message that Matt is claiming total responsibility, and that everything is all right. He is continuing to grow and mature where he is now, and is still quite interested in life. Nothing was lost because of this friend's actions."

My guest promised to share the recording of our message circle with this friend to ease his mind. I just loved how he burst into a family meeting because of his compassion for his surviving friend. He didn't apologize for his actions, yet he took responsibility for them, and did his best to free his friend from guilt.

Spirit people may come through showing terrible physical or emotional pain. They may come through showing themselves as victims of violence, or suffering devastating illness. But they always rush to assure us that they are not now experiencing any pain at all. It is simply a method to identify themselves to the physical guests. When we hear a spirit's name it's a wonderful connection, but when we also hear about the details, what they were suffering from or what suffering they caused, the experience is more concrete for the living. My clients leave our sessions knowing for sure that they have just been with a loved one in spirit, and that's the whole point of these communications after all.

CHAPTER 10

Are They Truly All Right Where They Are?

I frequently forward the message that our spirit people are quite all right where they are. They respond with eagerness when a guest recognizes them, and are happy to spend some time conversing back and forth, through me. Yet they also seem to know that this kind of communication is only temporary, so most are quick to point out before they leave that they will meet their physical friends one day in the future.

A forty-ish woman came for an appointment one day with her friend. As I tuned in, I felt the presence of a young woman who'd passed before her time in a vehicle accident. My client acknowledged her daughter, who had died at the age of nineteen while traveling to a camping weekend with friends. The spirit conveyed her joy at her mother's presence, and insistently repeated that she really was safe and happy. Her younger sister needed to hear this message in particular, and she urged her mother to pass it on.

"Do you miss us?" the mother asked. "Do you think about us and miss us, are you counting the days till we can be together again, too?"

With a feeling of frustration from the spirit, I had to translate, "I'm fine!" yet again. This spirit came across as being almost dismissive of her family's grief. As her mother cried on my couch, the spirit came through very much like a teenaged girl, saying "Oh Mom, come on! I'm fine!"

After we concluded, I spent some time in meditation asking for help. How could I translate a spirit's genuine well-being, without sounding dismissive myself? How could I show my clients that the spirit people are so certain of meeting again, that they rarely spend much time trying to convince us?

A picture unfolded for me, in response to my request. The spirit people showed me that they do not experience time the way we do; where they are, all things happen at once. They are still here now, and they'll be together with loved ones in the future, which is really also right now.

Hard to imagine that we don't have to wait for things, I silently commented. *How can I get this concept across to grieving people—parents in particular?*

I began to see an airliner, traveling through the night sky. On board I saw that some of the people were awake, and some were asleep. The spirit people said I was seeing something that might help me explain the situation to my clients.

How does this explain it? I asked.

They told me: if you fly from New York City to Sydney, Australia, it is a long flight. Time and distance seem inherently connected. If you stay awake for the entire flight, you will begin to notice feelings of discomfort, boredom, impatience, and probably a desire to keep checking your watch, or your progress on the map. You may distract yourself with meals, cocktails, the in-flight movie, and strolls up and down the aisles to stretch your legs. Some people may find the whole business so aggravating that the entire flight is unpleasant.

If you fall asleep when the plane takes off, and don't wake again until the plane is landing, you have still covered the same amount of ground, but you have escaped the experience of time. You have simply closed your eyes in one place, and opened them in the next. Time and distance are not connected.

The spirit people showed me that we physical beings tend to experience time like those in the first group, whereas spirit people exist outside of time, as in the second group. What is interesting about this example, they told me, was that in the end both groups of people end up in the same place. The spirit people showed me that they experience our reunion as if only an instant has passed. We here in the physical world, who miss and remember them, can end up aware of every passing moment and how uncomfortable it can be without them. And yet we, too, will eventually experience the joy of our reunion. Their suggestion to us is this: if you know we will be together in the end, but you also must live in the physical world with the dimension of time, then try to make it as comfortable as you can. Because the moment we reunite all pain and longing falls away, even for those of us who were uncomfortable up until that point. Even the most painful journey, once ended, seems like it took just an instant once you get to your destination.

Are They Our Guardian Angels?

"Can I ask you a question?" the very pregnant young lady asked, right at the end of our message circle. She'd been quiet through most of it, shyly validating when I had a message for her, but otherwise sitting silently or smiling to herself. I invited her to ask whatever was on her mind.

"I was in a very bad car accident several months ago," she said, "and not even the police can believe I survived. I felt as though someone had taken over the wheel and steered me out of the way. Was that one of my loved ones acting as my guardian angel?"

I tuned in, and very soon began to see a distinguished gentleman with steely gray hair, a handsome, strong-jawed face and a trim, lean physique. He showed me that he'd passed quite quickly due to a defect in his heart. He showed me the state of Maine, and that he was an engineer or an architect.

For a moment no one in the circle could place him. I waited, watching the guests query each other. Suddenly, one of the guests called out that she knew who he was. She said his name, Carl, and everyone nodded eagerly; he was a relative of the young lady's husband. I asked the spirit man to show me what he knew about the car accident.

"I see him as though he is sitting next to you in the front seat. He shows me throwing an arm around your neck and yanking you towards him, pulling your head down and covering you."

"That's true!" the young lady said. "Even though I had my seat belt on, I was found all the way over on the passenger side of the front seat with my head down. I remember feeling as though someone pushed me."

"He shows me that he didn't take the wheel, but rather pulled you away from it."

"Yes! I felt like it was torn out of my hands, that's why I thought someone had grabbed the wheel!" she said.

When I asked the spirit if he was her guardian angel, he told me no, that he just happened to be there. I told them he had an interest in seeing this young lady survive, because the child she was carrying was going to have the same name as his.

The whole crowd burst out laughing because it was true; the boy she was due to deliver within weeks had already been named Carl. The yet-to-be-born baby did indeed share a first name with the spirit who'd passed away.

While I don't believe our spirit people act as guardian angels on a full-time basis, I do believe they will step in when given the opportunity to call our attention to something, or even to prevent harm. No spirit person has ever impressed upon me that they are now fully devoted to protecting a living person. I have seen that they participate in family events and even offer advice. I've seen, as in the example above, where they create something in the physical world. But I haven't seen that spirit people have any more ability to protect us, than any physical person in our presence. For instance, Carl in spirit was able to do perhaps what a living person might have done, had he been sitting in the passenger seat. Carl could not, in spirit, step in front of the moving cars and deflect them from one another.

At that same circle I gave a message to a woman for someone who was still alive. It was a very unusual kind of message, because I immediately felt as though my neck was broken. Searing pain and stiffness radiated from my neck, and I felt it had happened to a young man in a car accident. When I described what I was feeling, the woman seated across from me said, "Yes, I know who you're talking about, but he's still alive. He had an awful car accident, and broke his neck, but he did survive."

"I feel such terrible stiffness and pain here," I said, indicating the right side of my neck.

"He has pins in the vertebrae in his neck; he has very little mobility there, and he lives with chronic pain," she replied.

"And this guy's alive? Are you sure?" I said aloud, while silently I was thinking, *What the heck is going on here?*

She assured me he was alive, so I did what I always do in that situation—I waited. A silent minute or two passed while I parsed the impressions that were now coming in.

"I have a man in spirit, he has a name that begins with a C or a G, I'm not quite sure which letter I'm seeing. There is a name in common with someone he wants to give this message to. He gives me the feeling of being a father. Is this your father?" I asked her.

"No," she answered, looking very surprised, "but that's the father of the young man with the broken neck. The father's name is either Chris or George, and the son who is still alive is Chris, and his middle name is George."

"Did you know this father had passed away?" I asked, because the spirit person conveyed to me that she didn't know.

"No I didn't, but it isn't a surprise. He was very sick for a long time."

"Are you in contact with his son? I can't imagine why he is coming through in our reading, unless he would like you to pass a message on to Chris."

"Yes," she answered, "we're friends."

"Chris's father wants to warn him, that unless he is ready to be a father in the near future, he needs to be very, very careful. He wants him to tell him to be responsible or to look at the responsibility. Please pass that message on."

The guest paused for a moment before responding. "Chris is dating a single mother of a small child," she told me. "She is feeling that things are getting very serious, but I'm not sure he feels the same way."

"I'm not sure what the spirit father is addressing, but please pass on that Chris may become a father if he is not careful with birth control. Or it may be that he isn't aware of the responsibilities of being a father to the little child of his girlfriend."

She promised to pass the message on, and I'm sure when Chris hears it he'll know what his father is referencing.

If Chris's father were truly a guardian angel, wouldn't he just prevent an unwanted pregnancy, rather than warn Chris about being responsible? I'm not sure, but the spirit people have shown me that this sort of intervention is the manner in which they watch over us.

Can They Possess You or Control You?

Despite the drama of Hollywood and television, it has been my experience that spirit people cannot control a living person. Spirit people may show up unbidden, but when asked to leave, they always must and always do. Remember my incident with the two pilots in my living room? That was when I learned that I have total control over who comes through to me.

In New York City many years ago, I was taking the third in a series of four psychic development classes. Our wonderful instructor was Stephen Robinson, who is a practicing psychic and teacher. I made leaps and bounds in my own abilities under his tutelage. One morning we began our day with a deep meditation, which focused on opening our chakras one by one. Just minutes into this wonderful exercise, I was feeling blissful yet alert, when suddenly my Polish great grandfather showed up! My "dziadek" (as we called him), had passed away when I was a little girl, and it had been years since I'd even thought of him. Yet here he was, looking as I always remember him: white hair brushed back, barrel-chested, affectionate in a gruff, old-world kind of way. I was delighted to see him. I never once had, ever, since he'd gone out to the spirit world, yet I was also keenly interested in following the meditation in class. I didn't want to miss out on anything Stephen was teaching us.

I said, "Dziadek, go away! Not now!" and he vanished in an instant. I regret the abruptness with which I sent my great grandfather away, as he has never returned. I've petitioned my spirit guides and invited him, yet he has not come back to me. Perhaps he only had enough energy to get through once, or perhaps that particular vibration on that day allowed him to come through. My dziadek had appeared uninvited, and I'd asked him to leave. If a beloved family member can be banished that quickly, how could an unfamiliar spirit ignore a command to go away?

Even though I've set up the rules for working with the spirit people, it doesn't mean they won't take an opportunity to visit. As I mentioned in an earlier chapter, I used to work out at a local gym, ending my exercise routine with a cool-down stretch and a ten minute meditation. One morning, the gym was more crowded than usual, forcing me to find a different spot to cool down. Tucked into a corner behind the stair-climbing machines, I finished my stretch and began my meditation, but it was hard to concentrate in this new area. I was trying to clear my mind, but I just couldn't seem to settle in to mental relaxation. In addition, I had this nagging thought to open my eyes and look up.

After a few minutes I said to myself, "Oh, forget it," and opened my eyes. A woman in spirit was standing beside a young woman with her back to me on a stair-climber, directly in front of me. The spirit looked to be about middle-aged, and she showed me the cancer ribbon over her right breast. She indicated that it was her daughter on the stair-climber. I felt a surge of energy, and almost an unstoppable compulsion to inform the daughter that her mother was present in spirit. I even began to get to my feet when I thought, "Wait a minute. I'm not going over to that stranger to start talking about spirit people to her. She'll think I'm nuts!"

Still, I found myself rising to a standing position and being almost pulled over. I gave a stern look to the spirit person and said, "No. If your daughter is interested in looking for this connection, it's up to her to find a way to do it. Please go," and I sat back down. When I looked up again the spirit was gone, and I felt sure that I'd done the right thing. Though the mother in spirit had just shown up and tried to convince me to get her daughter's attention, in the end she had to respect my decision to be left alone. We living people always have the last word, even though spirit people can be very compelling with their impressions or energy.

During one of my stints at the New York Renaissance Faire, I had an interesting experience that I can only compare to stories I've read about channeling. A woman sat down at my little table in the woods for a fifteen minute reading, and I began as usually did, by asking for something of hers to hold. Within a short time, I felt the presence of a very strong-willed man in spirit, who she was able to identify as a former sweetheart.

"Was he really forceful in life? Because I have to tell you, he just busted in here, and is dominating my impressions completely!" I said to my client.

"Oh yes," she said, "that sounds like him." I went on to tell her that I felt enormous passion from him for her, of a very dramatic and demonstrative sort. I was chatting away about him while she tearfully smiled and validated, when suddenly I felt pushed sideways out of my chair. I looked to my right to see who had so rudely bumped into me, and I saw myself! There I was, right beside myself, as if my consciousness went from being behind my eyes to being about three feet to the left. I was in my body in the sense that I could still feel myself sitting on the chair, but the feeling was farther away, or separate from my sense of self. This guy had just bumped me out of my own body so that he could get closer to his sweetheart.

Boy, was I mad! I remember saying to him, *"MOVE!"* and suddenly I was back where I belonged. I scolded him vehemently right then and there, out loud, while my client gaped at me. I told him to back up and stand farther away from me, and when I wanted to—*if* I wanted to—I'd start taking his impressions again.

I explained what was going on to my client, who seemed both amused and unsettled by his behavior. "I guess people don't really change much when they pass away," she said. "He was so much like that in life, throwing his weight around and kind of bullying people."

"Well that's not going to work with me," I told her, and continued on sharing my psychic impressions about her future. As our fifteen minutes came to an end, I felt the impression of a plaintive little tug on my right sleeve. With a sheepish kind of energy, the male spirit cautiously came forward. I allowed a connection between us so I could pass on a final message. This time he was respectful, gentle with his energy, and very loving towards his sweetheart.

Thinking I'd made my point, I relaxed a little more, to let more of his energy impress itself on me, when I felt him push me again. He seemed to shove his right arm down into mine from my shoulder to my fingertips, as if my arm were a glove he was putting on. It felt as though my awareness of my arm was squeezed to the inside of my skin, and it became his energy, neurons and motor skills that lived in my arm. It felt as though I had a perfectly normal arm attached to my body, but which belonged to someone else. Faster than I'd thought possible, he (using my arm) reached across the table, snatched up her hand, and brought it to his lips, which were somewhere over my right shoulder. Thankfully he didn't bring her hand to my lips!

Just imagine how this looked. My arm shot across the table, grabbed her hand, pulled it up to somewhere in the air next to the right side of my head, and then flung it back down again. This all happened before I could even process what was going on, and I don't know who was more surprised, my client or myself. He vanished quickly, I suspect to avoid another scolding from me. When I told the woman what had just happened, her face lit up in a huge smile. Apparently, he always used to kiss her hand.

I was a fairly naive psychic when that incident happened, and looking back I'm surprised I wasn't so unnerved that I quit right then. But I was mad at that spirit's rudeness more than anything else, which gave me the focus and energy to put him in his proper place. That was the only time anything like that ever happened to me, and it wasn't long afterwards that I began to set rules which the spirit people must comply with, if they want to work with me. Because those rules are now part of my process, even the spirits who show up early for message circles respectfully wait where I ask them to—on the porch.

Neither of these incidents I describe were possession, because I remained in total control. All it took was a firm word to remind the spirit person that no matter how excited he was to contact his living loved one, he had to respect not only my person, but my desire to make or not make the connection. Of course, there are times when I'm not expecting a spirit person, but will deliver a message anyway. Those times are few and far between. I compare it to someone coming for an appointment. A person can't just show up at my door and force me to meet with him or her right away. If I'm not busy, and I feel like it, I might rarely say "Yes," but I'd almost always say "No," because there are rules and boundaries to be respected.

Do They Haunt Places

Opinions vary on this subject, and, as with every topic connected to the supernatural, the only truly verifiable answer is, "Nobody knows." Television shows and movies about hauntings abound, some of which are documentaries attempting to prove the existence of a spirit. Some try to capture physical evidence through thermal detection equipment, special cameras, or audio recording equipment. I haven't personally seen any evidence of a haunting, nor have I been overwhelmingly convinced after watching any of those documentaries. But I have had some odd experiences that I don't really know how to categorize.

The Merriam-Webster dictionary defines "haunt" this way: *To visit or inhabit as a ghost* and *to appear habitually as a ghost.* The word "haunt" doesn't mean to appear in spirit at a message circle, or during a reading, or even to show up at the gym and stand next to a cardio machine. It means that a spirit person actually lives in, or habitually visits, a particular place. If most haunting stories are to be believed, it's usually a place where the physical person died a tragic or unjust death. Not only that, the spirits are generally believed to be unable to rest, or go home to heaven or God. You may be interested to know that the word "haunt" originates from the Old Norse *heimta,* which means "to lead home" and *heimr,* which means "home."

I certainly believe spirit people exist—I work with them everyday and I'm completely convinced that they're capable of communicating with us. I've heard far too many cries of validation to conclude that spirit people aren't real. Yet, I don't believe that spirit people roam the earth unsettled, stuck here due to a tragic death, unrequited love, or bent on revenge.

In my experience, as you've seen if you've read this far, spirit people come to visit us from time to time, but have really all gone to heaven. My guides, my ancestors, and the spirit people I meet, continually affirm that everyone gets to God, so I cannot reconcile the idea of haunting with my experience of the spirit world.

Not too long ago, an acquaintance asked me this very question. She and her family were just moving into an historic home in a nearby town. It was built in the mid-1800s and had served first as a private home, and then as an inn. Before moving in, she'd gone over to take some pictures of the rooms in the house, which she could refer to while shopping for paint colors and furniture. She called me when she found multiple orbs of light in almost all of the photographs, but most abundantly in the those pictures taken of a small bedroom. She and her husband had also pried up a floorboard after tearing out an old rug, and found a lady's button-up shoe, a child's block, an apothecary bottle, and a whiskey bottle. At her invitation, I went over to see if I could pick up on anything.

Never having done something like this before, I decided I'd approach it as I would a message circle. That is, I would sit down, say a prayer, close my eyes, and then just start talking about what came through. We sat down in the room in question, and I found myself welcoming spirit people in almost immediately. Holding on to the shoe I met a wonderful woman in spirit who impressed upon me that she was a member of the extended family, and lived there in her late middle-age, working to help pay her way. Her feet hurt, her hips and knees hurt, and her favorite way to wind down was to sit in the rocking chair. However, the man of the house had informed her that if paying guests were staying at the inn, they got first dibs on the chair. She claimed to be delighted that the new tenants had brought in a rocking chair, so I informed my acquaintance that she could expect to hear or see that chair rocking.

Several other people came through, including the proprietor. He was a rigid, miserly type, who had enough to support his family in more comfort than he insisted they live. He took enormous pride in the addition he built, and the self-discipline with which he maintained his good health. An adolescent son of the family claimed that he and his cousin had taken the whiskey bottle from an older African man, who worked odd jobs where he could find them.

Each of these spirit people came through describing a bit of their lives at a certain time. For instance, the adolescent boy hadn't perished as a boy—he just came through that way because of the context of the whiskey bottle. The rigid, austere man of the house came through as he did in the context of the apothecary bottle, which he said contained a tonic he regularly drank for his health. In general, I got a sense of excitement from the spirit people that a family was moving in. I even got the sense that these spirit people might pop in from time to time, but I did not sense that they were stuck there, or were haunting the old inn. It remains to be seen whether any of this information can be validated, as my acquaintance hopes to do some research into the family who owned the place.

A few other times I've run into spirit people who seem to turn up in the same place rather regularly. The first time, I was in college. The man I was dating lived a few towns away in the attic of a house that had been divided into three apartments. He woke up more than once to find his dirty dishes washed or his laundry folded, swearing he hadn't done it himself. His roommates told similar stories about plants moving on the table, or shoes being moved from the hallway to a mat beside the door. I didn't really believe their stories, as none of them had ever seen the spirit that was helping three single guys keep their place neat. I hoped for an experience of my own, though in the back of my mind I didn't really think it was possible. I'd heard about seeing ghosts, but had never heard about ghosts that moved things or did chores.

One sunny winter afternoon I sat in the kitchen by myself, while the boys were outside in the driveway working on a friend's truck. I was watching them out the window in a lazy, day-dreamy sort of way, when I reached into my pocketbook for a cigarette. As I brought a match to my mouth to light it, the ashtray at the other end of the table slid across to me and stopped right at the edge, where I hesitantly dropped the match. I said a quiet "thank you," to no one I could see, and ran outside to be with the others. I'd be lying if I said I wasn't momentarily freaked out. That sort of thing can be downright startling, and I didn't have any of the training or experience I have now. That was the first time I experienced the physical evidence of someone I could not see, and unfortunately I wasn't able to explore that place much more. My guy and I split and moved on, so I never learned who was there or why he was so interested in keeping the attic apartment neat.

Years ago I rented office space in an old building near the center of town. It was there that I first began conducting open message circles, to which anyone who reserves a seat is welcome for a modest fee. At every circle I conducted there, I was aware of a very young Union soldier standing at attention behind me and to my left, in a corner of the room. He never came forward or spoke to me, and I knew he wasn't an ancestor of any of the guests who came. The building wasn't old enough to have existed during the Civil War, so I concluded he wasn't attached to the structure. I never saw him during regular one-on-one readings, or at any other time I was alone in my office. He only impressed his presence on me during my monthly open circles. None of the other tenants felt that building was haunted when I discreetly poked around. I once asked him about himself and he didn't answer. I understood then that he wasn't taking questions and was simply there watching. Was he haunting the place? I don't think so. I believe he just took an interest in what was going on in a message circle atmosphere. Perhaps he was on assignment from the spirit world, or learning about spirit communication on his end of the line.

Hiking through the woods with my dog recently, I saw another Union soldier. We were near the Appalachian Trail in a very historic area of the Hudson Highlands, across the river from West Point. Though I'd been to explore some of the old mines, forges, and homesteads, I'd never become aware of any spirit people. This guy was a total surprise. I actually thought he was real, because many local groups reenact historic battles here. I was walking that morning, again in a very day-dreamy state of mind, when fifty feet away to my right I noticed movement through the trees. In my peripheral vision I saw a man who'd been squatting with his back to me, suddenly stand up and turn around to face me. In a moment it became clear that he was a spirit person, so I kept him in my peripheral vision, rather than looking directly at him. I've found that when I look directly at where a spirit seems to be, they vanish from my mind's eye, as my physical eyes register what's actually there in the three-dimensional landscape.

He looked a bit frightened, and I felt at once that he had run away, or that he wasn't with his unit like he was supposed to be. He looked as though I'd surprised him, and I sensed that he didn't know what to do. I smiled to myself and moved on, and after he disappeared from my peripheral vision I turned back to look. Of course, there was no sign of him. I've hiked there many times in that same mental state, and never met that soldier before. Was he haunting the woods where he'd hidden out? I don't know, but I hope one day I'll see him again so I can invite him for a chat.

A former teacher once gave me this analogy: like the character Pig Pen in the old Charlie Brown comic strips, we leave a little bit of ourselves, our energy, everywhere we go. I suspect this is why my cat loves to sleep on my desk chair, though there are several other more comfortable chairs in the house. It's why we tend to gravitate towards the same chair in a classroom or the same pew in a church. I believe whatever we see, feel or hear in a so-called haunted room, is really just the leftover energy of the former inhabitants, but not the inhabitants themselves. And perhaps it's true that someone who died tragically leaves behind a more intense energy stain, which sensitive people can pick up from the environment.

The only honest answer I can give about whether or not spirits haunt places, is a humble "Nobody knows." Though I guarantee it'll all become clear when we're dead!

CHAPTER 11

Will They Ever Come Back?

Not everyone believes in reincarnation, so this can be a delicate question to answer when a client asks, "Will my loved one come back to earth before I die? If so, will I miss them when I get to heaven?"

Personally, I do believe that we can choose to be reborn. I was raised a Catholic and didn't believe in reincarnation until I had a past life regression that saved my life. Shackled by an eating disorder for more than a decade, I had nearly given up on recovery. After trying everything else, at the end of my rope, I went for a past life regression. In one two-hour session I was completely cured. I walked away from that experience knowing I had some serious studying to do, and embarked on a mostly self-directed, years-long education. There wasn't a whole lot written about reincarnation back when I had my first regression, nor was the internet a common household research tool. I read everything—and I mean everything—I could find on the subject. I took every multiple-lives class that cropped up in New York City, where I was living. I practiced on myself, my friends, and finally on volunteers, until I had a sufficient body of knowledge and personal experience to craft a full-fledged belief in reincarnation.

When I began to study hypnosis as a way to access past-life memories, I learned something quite remarkable: the subconscious mind records everything that ever happened to us, just like a video camera. This is why hypnosis can be used (following very strict protocol, and not in every State, nor in every trial) for witness testimony. In other words, whether or not we have a conscious recollection of making a memory is immaterial; everything we perceive is being stored in the subconscious mind. Everything, from the moment life begins. If you believe life begins at conception, that's where your subconscious mind hits the Record button. If you believe life begins at birth, your memories start there. For those of us who believe that we've lived before, it's through the memories stored in the subconscious mind that we can recall a previous life.

Since I began studying reincarnation I have regressed more than one thousand clients to one or more past lives. I myself have experienced several regressions, with three that stand out as life-changing. One of the techniques I developed involves asking my clients questions about what happens in between their lives. Dr. Michael Newton has written extensively on life between lives, and I recommend his books highly (see the Resources section).

Spirit people often mention that they'll be waiting for someone, or say things like "I'll meet you when you're coming out," or "I'll see you here." In a recent message circle, a spirit father came through for one of the guests, with a message for her estranged brother, whom I'll call Tom. We were all a bit perplexed, as my guest and her brother hadn't spoken to each other in many years. The spirit person finally mentioned Tom's wife Beryl, with whom my guest had once had a warm association. With the message "Beryl needs you," I thought I'd concluded our business with that spirit person. However, before the circle ended, the spirit father came back and said that he'd been waiting for Tom, and would be escorting him soon. He said, "Beryl needs to know that I waited for him, and will show him what to do. She needs to know he won't be alone."

A few months later my guest called to tell me she'd heard from Beryl that her brother Tom had passed away. Beryl recognized that some of Tom's behavior had alienated him from most of the family, and she was doubly saddened that he was alone in his illness, and that the funeral was poorly attended. She was concerned that he would be alone in the afterlife, too. My guest was able to tell her the message from their father, which greatly eased her sister-in-law's heart.

Theories abound about the size of the soul, whether just a small part comes down into the human body and most remains in the spirit world, or whether we have an over-soul that guides our smaller souls in the body. Dr. Newton's research is a great place to start to formulate your own answers to these questions. As for me, I believe we leave a part of ourselves in the spirit world where we have low activity levels while we incarnate in the physical realm. In my work as a medium, every adult spirit who has come through says they'll "be here" when their loved ones cross over. I believe that our loved ones, or at the very least a recognizable part of their energy, will meet us when we go out.

On many occasions I meet little babies who didn't make it into the world, due to abortion, stillbirth, or miscarriage. A few times these little spirit people will mention that they're coming back in to try again through the same parents or to another close family member. I have never heard one say that they have come back in already, as someone else.

What Do They Say About Heaven?

In order to get a message to one of their physical family during a reading, the spirit people have to make some sort of impression on me, as the medium. To do that, they have to stir up in me something that I can identify or recognize. As I mentioned earlier, a spirit person won't come to me speaking Portuguese, as I don't understand this language. Instead such a spirit would show me a map of Portugal, give me a taste of Madeira wine, or impress some other picture or feeling that would cause me to say to myself, "Aha! Portugal!"

When it comes to describing their heavenly environment, the spirit people not only have to find something similar in my vernacular, but they also want to convey something recognizable to their physical family. In one memorable reading, my client's father came through saying he was with Jesus, which was thrilling news to his daughter. She herself was a lapsed Catholic, but she recalled how devoted her father was to Jesus, especially in his later years. In another reading, a sister in spirit came through describing a celestial meadow, filled with the horses she'd owned and loved in her younger life. To my physical client, knowing her sister was exactly where she'd want to be, as she had often described "heaven on earth," was an enormous comfort.

Is heaven what we hope it will be? I don't know. Each spirit who chooses to touch on the subject, describes a place that triggers immediate recognition in my physical client ("Oh yes! That's exactly how he knew heaven would be!"), fitting in with what the spirit believed when alive in the physical, and what the loved one hoped for him. Perhaps that means heaven is whatever we need or desire it to be at any given moment, or perhaps it so defies description that the spirit people placate us by describing such beautiful, peaceful settings.

What I do know is something the spirit people have told me repeatedly. There are no different levels of heaven. Every single spirit person who has commented on his environment has insisted that there is no class system in the spirit world. I'm sure many mediums will disagree with me. I've read books and case histories from some quite famous psychic mediums who say something entirely different. Yet, I have translated the oneness of the heavenly environment so many times, to so many different clients, from so many different spirit people, I'm beginning to conclude it's true. Criminals, suicides, unbaptized babies, cheating spouses, estranged family members... every single one of them says something like "We're all here together."

In some of the books I've read by other psychic mediums, I've seen descriptions of different levels of heaven. That suggests to me that some people don't make it there on their first try, or have to work off some bad behavior before ascending up the ladder to true peace and joy. I've read that some very terrible people spend years in a coma-like state, in darkness, until some moment in time when they're allowed to either come back to earth and live a life as a victim of someone such as they had been, or to work extensively with spirit guides in order to get their next life right. I've read that people who commit suicide wander the earth until they've lived out as many years as they were supposed to if they hadn't killed themselves. Yet in all the readings and message circles I've conducted, not once has a spirit person described being in limbo, purgatory, or hell. Not once has a spirit person said he is with spirits like himself, criminals or suicides, while all the happy saint-like spirit people are somewhere else. I've acted as a medium for multiple suicides, several criminals, and more abusive or cruel humans than I care to count. Every single one of them has come through with an acknowledgement of poor behavior or decisions, and with the message that they are with family and friends in heaven.

To some people, this might be extremely upsetting. Why should they have to spend eternity with someone they hate, or someone who abused them? I challenge those people to consider that they're not going to be in heaven with Hitler. He isn't being rewarded for his atrocities by going to heaven. That man was a spirit person who came down into the human body of Adolf Hitler, born into a human family, who lived in a human world filled with fear, competition, and misunderstanding. He was arguably the most terrible person in recent history. Of course, Adolf Hitler has never come to me during a reading or a circle, but I imagine if he did, it would be to acknowledge his heinous actions and to say, "I didn't understand, but I do now." From my experience—and that is all I reference—once we pass out of the human condition and go out to the spirit world, something extraordinary expands in our awareness, something that causes us to say, "Oh! I get it now!"

I remember in particular one reading I had with a fifty-ish woman. She'd come for psychic guidance more so than messages from spirit people, so for most of our session I answered her questions about her future. Near the end of our hour, a very strong female spirit came through, followed by a very meek male spirit. I asked her if I could connect her with them, and with her permission began to describe what turned out to be her mother and her father, both of whom she hated and resented.

"Your mother comes through with a real edge; she feels very angry, almost unstable with this raw, angry energy," I began.

"That sounds just like her. Why is she here? She hated me and treated me like dirt when we were growing up. She's the last person I want to hear from," was my client's disgusted reply.

"There is also a male spirit who is barely speaking up, he seems very timid or shy," I continued.

"That's my father. My mother abused us and he did nothing about it. I have nothing to say to him either. And I can't believe they're together. They hated each other, I have no idea why they stayed married. Are they just torturing each other in the afterlife, too?" Good question. I asked it silently of the spirit parents.

Her mother acknowledged how awful she'd been as a mother, and then began to define what was clearly mental illness that had gone undiagnosed. She did her best to send a refreshing kind of love and new understanding to her daughter. Her mother conveyed that, while alive, she had no way of realizing she was ill, or how to get out of her own damaged mindset. Her father acknowledged his flaws, too, and together they both showed great love for each other and my client. It was hard for my client to accept, though I hope over time the message will continue to reverberate with her, and she can find forgiveness.

Remember that judgment, the act of defining something as good or bad, right or wrong, is a human behavior. Once we leave our bodies, egos, and habits, once we go out from the physical world, those human behaviors don't apply anymore. The spirit people come through with their personalities intact, but usually that's just a way to help their physical loved ones to identify them. Even the bitterest, crankiest human being, once in the spirit world, has an entirely different, non-human perspective that we down here can't really grasp. So he or she might come through with a familiar flawed character, and once identified or validated by the client, acknowledge those flaws and then describe a new understanding.

According to the spirit people I have met, heaven seems to be a place where all of our flaws or so-called sins are swept away in the light of genuine understanding, and once we are washed clean of them, we are left with only love, compassion and joy. The spirit people say heavenly reward isn't parceled out in different amounts, because there is no judgment there.

Do They Ever Talk About God?

The spirit people I've met haven't talked about God per se; what they most often talk about is what they'd believed God to be when they were here in the physical world. The most consistent message that comes through, is that where they are there is no judgment, either from on high or from themselves. They tell of freedom, understanding, peace, and reunion with loved ones. Getting into the spirit world seems to be one huge "Aha!" moment, which will make total sense to us, too, when we're dead.

At the end of recent message circle for a family of sisters and cousins, a female in spirit came through.

"She comes through as very devout," I began. "She shows me a cross, so she maybe was a nun, or had been a nun. Do you know a Theresa who was a nun? This is a 'T' name." No one answered.

"Did any one of you ladies go to Catholic school?" I asked.

"Yes," two of the sisters answered.

"I feel like she's a nun, with a feeling of being like Sister Theresa." The women discussed among themselves who this person could be, and came up with a name of a nun they had known named Alma. The name gave me a *zing*, but it didn't reconcile with the name I felt I was receiving. I waited for more to develop.

"Do you, or does your family have a connection to St. Theresa?" I asked.

"Oh, yes! That's the name of the Catholic school we went to," one of the sisters offered.

"Was Alma a nun at that school?"

"No."

"Okay, well she's giving me the feeling of being a nun and also the name Theresa. So this spirit person is making a connection somehow, and I'm not sure yet what she means to say." I asked the spirit person in my mind why she was coming through with the name of their school, if she wasn't connected to it. I knew I definitely had a nun with me, and I figured she was showing me a school to underscore that she was more than just a devout layperson. Yes, she was most definitely a nun.

"She shows me now the Sacred Heart of Jesus... " I began.

"That's the name of the next school we went to—Sacred Heart!" cried one of the sisters.

"So she's talking about this tradition that she has, or referring to the one you came up in, and she says (and this is what she's making me say, not the words she would have used), she says 'sometimes you have to shovel a lot of shit before you get to what's really important.'" That message got a lot of laughter.

"She shows me a shovel and a pile of manure. She would not have said that, but she's making me laugh and getting me to say it. Her point is, it's not all that serious. That God is really playful. Spirituality is really playful. We are playful people. Sometimes in this tradition— or in any tradition whether it's Jewish or Christian—if we grow up with this ponderous, sort of somber seriousness about *GOD,* we lose sight of the playfulness and creativity that makes us who we are. So she's talking about her understanding where she is now, having had that tradition and having seen you guys go through that tradition, that it's really a lot more fun, and not to take ourselves so seriously. Not even to take God that seriously, that this is a fun relationship we can have that can be really enjoyable, and not one where we have to cover our heads and say 'oh I'm really sorry, please forgive me,' and always go confessing." This was news to me, having grown up a Catholic myself, so I asked for more from the nun in spirit.

"She says we can have more of a playful dialogue, so she's inviting you to invite God in, in a different sort of a way. It doesn't have to be 'Sunday we go to church' or we just say our prayers at bedtime or something like that, but to invite God in, in a more general, playful kind of way, and you're going to find that life is a lot more fun."

"That was a good message," offered one of the cousins.

"She knows, because she spent her physical life one way, and now she has a whole other feeling about God. Not that there's anything wrong with tradition, but there's more to it than that."

Do They Believe One Religion is Better Than Another?

Many nuns, ministers, devout laypeople, and even a monsignor in the Catholic church have been of one voice when it comes to religion. Every one has said, "there are many paths to God." I had a spirit nun come to a message circle with a message for a woman who was recently undergoing a change in her own practice of faith. She had been raised in a traditional Christian belief system and was exploring a different discipline. In particular, my guest had been questioning whether she was damaging her relationship with God by creating her own blend of spiritual practices.

The spirit nun spoke about balance in general at first, and then more specifically as it pertained to faith. "She's saying that there is something very lovely about marching to your own tune, and that the spirit people and the heavenly people look down with joy at a person's creativity in creating their own way to go forward [in the practice of faith], or in finding a balance that either comes from traditional, or is completely separate from traditional. She's encouraging the creativity and the balance in whatever direction you're considering going, as far as your faith or belief system or spirituality goes. This is looked upon with great delight by the people in the spirit world."

Encouraged by someone in-the-know, my guest breathed a huge sigh of relief and smiled throughout the rest of the evening.

Karma and Spirit Contracts

Karma is a subject too vast to cover in this book, but if it can be distilled down to one familiar adage, it would be "what goes around, comes around." In other words, you get what you give, and it can be day-to-day, it can span a lifetime, and, if you believe in reincarnation, it can be carried out across multiple lives.

A simple example of day-to-day karma happened to me a few years ago, and it was so crystal clear I have to laugh about it to this day. I'd recently moved from New York City to a suburban county and was taking the train back in to visit a friend. I'd gotten a later start than I'd promised—out of sheer laziness—but decided to blame it on a train delay. I told Regina that I'd be twenty minutes late, because there was an issue with the signals. We met up, had lunch, and went way downtown for some shopping. When it came time to head home, I hopped on the subway, planning to make the last train before rush hour. We'd just gotten underway towards Grand Central Terminal, when the subway train ground to a halt—and sat there for twenty minutes. Of course, I missed my train and had to spend more money to stand on a crowded car for the hour-long ride home, but I couldn't help laughing at myself and the perfection of my karma on that day.

Karma that spans over a lifetime may play out in ways we don't even notice. A child who bullies others may turn into an adult who develops a disability. A young woman who is unfaithful in her relationship may find herself betrayed in old age by a friend or family member.

Those who believe in reincarnation may find that current problems they're struggling with have a root in a previous lifetime. A greedy landowner who abused his tenants in fifteenth century France may struggle with prosperity in this life. These examples are just meant to illustrate that the concept of karma has not only to do with payback, but with our souls' instruction. We learn to be fully loving and compassionate when we can truly understand how another person feels. We might suffer in this lifetime to help balance our own karma, or the karma of ancestors or even strangers.

Some people believe that we make decisions about the kind of life we're going to lead, who our parents will be, what challenges or trials we'll face, before we're born. If we're a soul in the spirit world who has to balance some karma from a past life, we may decide with our spirit guides before incarnating that we'll face handicaps, abusive situations, or poverty.

At first I reserved an opinion about this concept, though I believed in karma. Over the years, as a regressionist and medium, I've seen enough examples of this pre-birth life-planning to make me a believer. One message from a spirit person stands out in particular. I'd never had this kind of contact before, so both my client Karen and I sat astonished as I translated what her spirit son said to us. She had asked during a psychic reading why she was unable to carry a child to term. She'd had three miscarriages and fertility treatments that had failed.

When I tuned in for her I said, "I feel like I see one spirit, so I feel like this is one spirit who made three attempts to come in, it wasn't three different children trying to find their way in. He gives me a masculine feeling. And I'm asking him why he didn't stay. I'm asking him if there is something physically that you did or didn't do. And this is what he's telling me, which is really unusual. He's telling me if he came in and grew up, he would have broken your heart. He shows me himself as if he were … he's showing me himself skiing, and I'm saying to him 'skiing?' but then he shows me 'ski bum,' and then just 'bum.' He shows me smoking, and not having a pleasant experience as an adult human being. He's telling me that you guys had agreed that he was going to come in and be this person to help him learn something, and he would help you learn something." I paused for a moment, then asked, "Do you believe in reincarnation?"

"I do," Karen answered me.

"He's giving me a feeling that there was a plan or agreement that he was going to come in and then would die during his very early adulthood, eighteen, nineteen, twenty years old, die this terrible, drug-addled death. The picture he's showing me, is him against a building, grungy, emaciated... just terrible. This is what he was going to come in and do, but at the last minute he couldn't do it. There was an agreement you made when you both were in the spirit world, that he was going to come in and pass away [as a young man] and you were going to learn something from that, but he's giving me the impression that he tried three times but each time he said, 'I can't do that to her,' and that's his answer as to why he didn't stick around. He's also telling me he's going to have to come in and do it anyway with someone at some other time, and you're still going to have to learn what he was going to help you learn, but he's saying 'I loved her too much, I couldn't do it.'

"He says that you didn't do anything wrong, you were holding up your end of the agreement by getting married and getting pregnant three times and going through fertility treatments. He says it was he who chickened out at the end. That's why there is no real medical reason why, it was just his choice not to hold up his end of the agreement, because it would be terrible for you."

"That's right," Karen said, "we couldn't find any medical reason why I could conceive but not stay pregnant."

"He shows me a picture and I feel like my heart is breaking when I see this young man who just didn't get it together, and is destroying himself, and I feel that this is what would have happened to you, and you would be feeling this heartbreak. I never got a message like that before, it's very interesting. It's very moving, because I always thought the agreements had to stick."

"So he would have come in and had a terrible time with drugs and died as a teenager?" she asked me.

"Yes, and he couldn't do it. He thought it was better not to come through, than to come through and make you suffer so much. He says you will know and recognize him when you get to the spirit world. He knew what the plan was before coming in and it all made sense from the spirit perspective, but once he got into the human tissue that was being created he began to consider what he was going to do from a human perspective and saw how painful it would be for you. I don't feel he backed out because he didn't want to do it, but because he

114

didn't want to do it to you. He says, 'that's how much I loved you.'"

My client went on to tell me that her family had a history of substance abuse and depression, perhaps even borderline mental illness on her mother's side, and that it wouldn't have surprised her if that gene had been passed down.

It was this spirit message in particular that cemented my belief in pre-birth contracts or agreements with other souls here in the physical world. I encourage you to explore these ideas yourself. When you know that even the most painful or challenging relationship was predetermined out of total love and desire to help teach an important lesson, it's so much easier to experience those relationships without judgment and with compassion.

PART FOUR

Messages From The Other Side

CHAPTER 12

The Message Circle

If you're going to a message circle or getting a reading for the first time, it helps to understand how the process works. Every psychic medium is unique and works differently, so when you're searching for a practitioner, be sure to ask her how she works and what, if anything, she would like for you to bring or to do. When I'm doing psychic readings, I like my clients to come prepared with some questions for us to focus on. Because our futures change with every decision we make, a client is likely to get vague answers when he or she asks, "where do you see me in five years." It's better to ask specific questions, such as "I don't know whether I should return to school for something different, or stay in the career I have." As you can see, you're not giving away any information to the psychic, but instead giving her a thread to follow into the future.

When it comes to spirit communication readings or message circles, I don't want to know anything about my clients. When I make the appointment, I take the first name only, and often don't know anyone's name in the group until we are all seated and ready to begin. I have no prior knowledge of my clients or guests when they walk into my office for the first time. In addition, I've trained myself to forget my clients immediately upon their departure, so if they come back again for another session I will have forgotten anything I said about them.

It's very important for me to present not only myself but my field as completely ethical, and those who come to me can be assured that whatever information that's coming through for them, comes from the spirit world and not from my memory of a previous reading. During the course of a message circle, I ask for guest's name for two reasons:

1. I forget it instantly, on purpose, and,
2. The sound of the guest's voice strengthens my connection to him.

It can seem pretty comical sometimes when I greet people at my door saying "Nice to meet you," and having them respond, "We've met twice before!" It can be equally humorous when I walk right by former clients in the street without recognizing them, only to have them stop me and say, "It's me! I was just at your house! You brought through my father!" To myself I think, "I swear I have never seen you before in my life. You were at my house?"

When the circle begins I let my guests know how I work, and what they can expect me to do and say. I remind them I'm not a trance channel—I don't absent my consciousness from the process. No spirit person inhabits my body or uses my vocal chords. This means the guests can get up and use the restroom if they need to, they can reach for tissues and blow their noses, and they can interrupt me if they have a question. The connection between me and the spirit world will not be broken. I tell them that because I'm predominantly clairsentient, I'm going to talk about feelings I get from the spirit people. I might feel as though I have tuberculosis, suicidal depression, or an amputation; I may feel that I'm in a car accident or on life support, overdosing on drugs, or lost in a fog of Alzheimer's. I hasten to assure my guests that their loved ones aren't suffering from these afflictions anymore, just using them as an identifier.

I inform the guests that I'm also clairvoyant. I tell them that when a visual impression comes to me, I will likely close my eyes, or turn my head to look at a blank wall. With clairvoyance, the impressions from our physical eyesight can overpower the impressions from the mind's eye, so I prepare them by saying "I may be giving you a message and suddenly close my eyes while I'm talking to you." I let them know I'm not going into any kind of trance when I do this, so they may continue to validate or ask me questions.

I also tell my clients that I don't want them to volunteer any details. If during a circle I hear someone say, for instance, "that could be my grandfather, but he didn't die of emphysema, he died of... ," I holler at them immediately before than can even finish the sentence. I say, "don't tell *me*, let me tell *you* how he died!" I ask that while they're settling themselves before the circle begins, not to discuss who they are hoping to hear from either, so that I don't even subconsciously pick up on anything.

I remind them to be open to all sorts of spirit people who might come through, not just the one or two that they most want to hear from. Spirit people will often send through a less emotionally significant spirit to connect with, as a way to break the ice. Once the guests experience that spirit communication and relax a bit, the more significant loved ones follow.

The key instruction I repeat to my guests before we begin, involves the importance of validating information that comes through. I tell them that the part of my mind that receives impressions is rather shallow; it seems to me that the spirit people can put one impression or symbol there at a time. When I share that with my guests it wipes the slate clean, and another symbol can come through. If a guest or client doesn't validate, I assume I've misinterpreted the symbol, and I dismiss it and ask the spirit person for another one. When five or six symbols or impressions aren't validated, I dismiss the spirit person altogether, asking them to try another tack to connect with me later on in the circle.

If a guest or client is testing me, as they sometimes do, they may miss an opportunity to connect with a spirit loved one. The following example actually happened in a circle one Spring evening in my home. I became aware of a spirit person and offered five specific impressions to a guest, by presenting:

- A female spirit who passed before her time,
- Showing the cancer ribbon around the area of her throat,
- Who gave me an "L" name like Linda or Lynn,
- Who felt as though she was very heavily medicated at the end of her life, so that communication was difficult, and
- Who showed me a DNA spiral, meaning that her disease appeared in a previous and/or subsequent generation...

The guest I was addressing did not validate or declare her knowledge of this spirit, so I assumed I missed the connection, and shut it down. We were getting ready to end for the night, when the guest in question suddenly said, "What about my mother?"

"What about her?" I asked.

"You had her here, what did she want to tell me?" The guest went on to confirm, almost two hours later, that the spirit with throat cancer was her mother, whose name was Linda. She actually told me she was testing me, because she was the first person I came to. She wanted to see if I could read other people first. This guest was afraid that the woman who made the appointment might have told me about her deceased mother.

With some effort I was able to recall the spirit mother, but the connection wasn't very strong, as the energy of the whole evening was dissipating. I was unable to bring in a specific message for her from her mother, other than the fact of her mother's presence. I know she left disappointed. No matter how I explain that validation isn't giving information away, there is still reluctance on some guests' part to acknowledge. Explaining the importance of validation is a major part of my introduction.

With my process explained and any questions answered, I turn on a recorder and start with a prayer, which usually goes something like this:

"Heavenly Father, Blessed Mother, I ask you to watch over us this evening. Open our hearts and minds to the wonders of Your love, keep us safe and free of fear, so that we may welcome and acknowledge our loved ones in spirit. Let these beautiful people assembled together leave here tonight with an absolute certainty that life is eternal, that love survives physical death, and that we will all meet again. Please watch over us this evening, as we get in our cars and travel home, and every morning as we get up and go about our day. Amen."

I then say my first name, and ask those seated around me to say their first names, too. It doesn't matter if I hear a nickname, full name, or the name in one's original language. I am concentrating on the sound of the guest's voice.

I take a minute or two with my eyes closed to note the most prominent spirits who come in, and I dash down a few notes. Then I begin dealing out the spirit people like cards, going around the group and leaving a verbal marker with each person before starting back at the beginning with more detail.

For example, I might start with the person at my right hand, and say, "There is a man here who shows me a heart attack, and next is a woman who shows me a cancer ribbon over her right breast. Next to her is a man in spirit who shows me smoking and having a machine breathe for him, then I see a little spirit who didn't make it into the world."

I'll continue around until all of the spirit people in the first wave of activity have been announced. I then return to the first person on my right, to fill in more details. Using the same example above, I would come back to the guest on my right and say something like, "This man in spirit shows me his heart, and that it was not the first time he had a heart attack. He shows me that he was outside mowing the lawn when he had the final one. He shows me himself in the hospital bed on machines while waiting for someone to fly in from somewhere;" Once this spirit has been recognized and validated, I deliver his message. It's not always this regular. Sometimes a particular spirit is more forceful than the others I've announced, and instead of returning to the first person I spoke to, I find myself addressing a different guest.

The spirit communication goes on in this fashion until I feel as though I have announced every spirit and delivered every message. At this time, spirits who came through earlier may come back with more to say. I'll know I'm complete with the spirit when the feelings they were giving me go away. A stroke victim will continue to give me a feeling of pain in my head, until I've made sure everything she wanted to say has been said. Even if she steps aside so I can bring through other spirits, she may give me that feeling of pain later on. I'll know she has more to contribute then, and I'll announce, "So-and-so's still here! Let's see what she has to say."

In general our message circles are fun, light-hearted, and very positive. Though there may be tears, they are usually tears of joy, relief, or laughter. Even those guests who approach the evening with trepidation, leave relaxed and unburdened. It's quite amazing to feel the energy in the room after a message circle, and instead of draining or tiring me, I often find myself so keyed up from the spirit energy that I have difficulty falling asleep.

What Do Spirits Know About Our Illness or Death?

I purposely avoid learning about anatomy and illness, so if a spirit person communicates about someone's health, I won't extrapolate. For instance, let's say I learned about diabetes and its cause, treatment, and cure. Then in a reading, if I get the feeling of diabetes I might be naturally inclined to pay attention to my conscious mind, which would very helpfully be offering up opinions about the cause, treatment, and cure. So while it's impossible to completely avoid knowing things about illnesses, I don't actively seek out information.

Last Spring, a wonderful couple and their two young daughters came in for a reading. The girls suffered from something I'll call Illness A; one girl had gotten it at three years old, and it had completely taken over her body. The other twin had gotten it earlier, but was manifesting a less severe case of it. I know nothing at all about Illness A, except I've heard the word and know what it's primary symptom is.

The couple had come in for a psychic reading to ask about their daughters' future (Illness A is not terminal by the way), whether I saw it reversing, and how that might happen. Though they hadn't come for spirit communication, during the reading I felt the presence of a female come stand next to the wife. This spirit was plump, apple-cheeked, held a rolling pin, had an "A" name, and showed me that she had had a stroke. When I conveyed all of this information, the wife identified the spirit as her brother-in-law's mother.

I asked the spirit why she had come, especially when more closely-related spirits might have come through. The spirit immediately drew my attention to what I modestly call "down there," and pointed to the wife. My client couldn't confirm that this lady had had issues in her reproductive organs. In fact, she felt quite certain that she hadn't had any problems there at all. But the spirit lady persisted. When I asked for clarification, the spirit showed me that my client had been to a specialist for her own irregular menstruation.

"I don't think she's indicating her own reproductive or sexual organs, but yours. I don't mean to be personal, but are you having, or have you had, difficulty in this area?" I asked.

"I did have problems there. I didn't get my period for four years," she said, "but I resolved that issue, and now everything's fine." I felt the spirit club me over the head with her rolling pin when the wife said she had "resolved that issue." My client continued on to say that she had been to a specialist. I was urged by the mother-in-law in spirit to ask more about this specialist, which I did.

"I went to a local Ayurvedic doctor," my client answered. When she said the word "Ayurvedic" the spirit person ramped up her vibration—gave me that *zing!*—and pointed at the daughters. When I get that ramped up vibration feeling, it's like a surge of delicious energy that runs through my entire body. I've come to identify this to mean, "Yes! You got it!" or "Yes! That's who I am!" So when this very patient spirit got us to turn our attention to Ayurvedic medicine, she was able to convey that she saw healing through this modality for the girls' illness.

"Have you tried an Ayurvedic approach with your daughters?" I asked. Apparently some time ago they had tried, but both husband and wife felt that the practitioner wasn't the right one for them. It now made sense why this barely-related spirit came through. She could get the wife to talk about resolving another health issue, and the spirit knew that this approach would also help the little girls. With that connection made, the exhausted spirit just seemed to vanish in an instant, leaving us to discuss this kind of treatment. Obviously we have to wait and see, but I believe this spirit came in direct response to my question—to the parents' question—about the best way to resolve Illness A.

Only on rare occasions have spirit people even referred to a living person's death, and in those instances the living people were already on their death beds. The spirit people are aware that a loved one is about to go out, and their message is that they will be there to meet them.

CHAPTER 13

Fetal Spirits

In almost every reading or message circle, I bring in a little person who describes herself as someone "who didn't make it into the world." When she is the first to come in, or if she comes in alone, I know that she is connected to my client. If she comes in in the company of another spirit person, she is usually attached to that spirit.

As you may imagine, miscarriage, and abortion in particular, can be very sensitive subjects. Whatever Catholic ideas I held about unbaptized babies, abortion, miscarriage, and stillbirth before my work as a medium, have all been stretched or completely reframed. This book is not intended to disseminate my beliefs, nor would I presume to lecture or convert my readers or clients to a different viewpoint. But I would be doing a great disservice to the spirit people if I didn't pass on the one message I always receive: "Just because I didn't make it into the world this time, doesn't mean I'm lost." Each little spirit seems so easy-going, as if to inform us that no harm was done.

So many of my women clients who have experienced a miscarriage, feel that they in some way contributed to it, either because of their personal biology, or because they did, or didn't do, something during pregnancy. One client had a bad argument with her then-husband, and miscarried a short time later. She felt certain that her acrimonious outburst had killed her baby. When the little fetal spirit came through to tell her that it had most certainly *not* been killed because of her high emotion, she was greatly relieved. The little one simply said, "I just didn't make it into the world. Nothing was lost or killed. We'll meet again."

A stillborn baby girl came through with the grandmother of one of my guests. The grandmother spirit was overjoyed to be coming in with this little spirit person, and acknowledged how the loss of this child had overshadowed her entire life and the lives of her other children. She acknowledged that she had spent too much time grieving, that she had retreated from living and loving because of this loss, and that it all became so clear to her when she met this baby in the spirit world. The little girl spirit was coming in with the same message, that she hadn't been lost or killed, she simply didn't come in at that time. As I was relaying this message to the young woman in our circle that evening, I was a bit surprised at my guest's emotional reaction.

"Does this message make sense to you?" I asked her.

"Yes, very much so," she said, nodding. I waited for more from her, but she just remained tearfully quiet. When I pass on a message that the guest acknowledges, she usually gives a bit of background as to why it's significant for her. If she doesn't elaborate, I understand that it's a deeply personal message, and I move on. Yet for some reason I didn't want to move on from this message, so I did what I'm sure you know by now I always do—I waited. Very slowly and quietly, as if the spirit people were deer in the woods, I saw the grandmother and stillborn spirits back away, and another spirit person come forward. She was so petite and timid, I felt as though I were watching a little fawn step cautiously out into an open area.

"There's another little spirit person here, who says she didn't make it into the world. She feels brand new and very small. The others have backed away, so I sense that she is connected to you, and not to your grandmother," I said. "You don't need to say anything, but I want to say that she's here and that she's all right, everything is just fine."

My guest began to cry in earnest now, nodding, her face covered by her hands. She acknowledged that several months ago she had miscarried—she thought it was because she'd had a sip of wine—and she'd been unable to overcome her grief and guilt. Her grandmother's message, and then the appearance of her own little spirit, allowed her to release herself from that personal torment and begin living again. By the time our circle ended her whole demeanor had changed. She was upbeat and clear, and seemed quite joyful.

I often have very similar experiences with fetal spirits who didn't come in to the world because of abortion. I don't distinguish the reason to my guests, though I can often sense whether a pregnancy ended due to abortion or miscarriage. As abortion can be a polarizing subject, and the guests in my open circles frequently don't know each other, I don't even ask for acknowledgment. But I will say that in my experience, unequivocally, those spirit people who did not make it into the world due to abortion come through with the exact same message: "Nothing was lost, nothing was killed. I just didn't come in at this time."

Early in my career I conducted an open circle at a New Age shop in another town. There were about a dozen people in attendance, who'd come in pairs or singly, from as far away as Florida. I'd read just about everyone, when a little fetal spirit appeared, and I made the mistake of saying she hadn't come in due to abortion. I didn't ask for acknowledgment from the guest, but went on to deliver the message that the little one hadn't been lost or killed. I said something like, "I don't know how anyone here feels about abortion, but I always get this message."

The middle-aged woman from Florida began gathering up her things in a mighty huff. She stood up so quickly that her chair scraped back loudly and fell over. Her husband leapt to his feet beside her. She began to berate us, me in particular, for supporting what she called the horrors of abortion, and let us all know she wouldn't spend another minute in the room with us. I followed her out of the room to talk to her and to ask her to return. After all, her own spirit people came through and she believed the messages they gave her—why wouldn't another spirit's message carry the same weight? But she wouldn't be mollified, and walked out. When I returned to the circle, I was mortified and deeply concerned about how my other guest, so newly freed from guilt, would be feeling. I had no need to worry, because when I went back inside she and the others were actually laughing!

The guest connected to the fetal spirit admitted that as a single woman she had had an abortion in her early twenties. For years she'd beaten herself up for it, and felt she had so abused God's trust that she'd never get to heaven. Hearing from the spirit itself allowed her to see the dangers of judgment, especially the damage harsh self-judgment can do. In an instant she was able to forgive herself. She said it was like a cloudy sky suddenly clearing. So when the Florida couple began their verbal attack, she saw it for what it really was: judgment. Instead feeling wounded, she felt instead compassion and relief. She would never speak to herself or anyone else that way again.

I know that each of us has the right to our own personal viewpoint. At the risk of another fire-storm, I will say only this: Let's learn from the spirit people themselves, and not judge anyone, or ourselves, too harshly. The need to judge others is a human condition, not a divine condition. Let's just take the message, learn our lesson, and move on.

CHAPTER 14

Children and Teenagers

Spirit people who have passed before their time, as children or teenagers, have come through in both private readings and message circles. In general, they have a great deal of energy and quite a sense of humor. I've seen these spirit children persist in their bid for acknowledgement far longer than adult spirit people.

The first time I ever set out to communicate with a spirit for another person was many years ago, under the guidance of my terrific teacher, Stephen Robinson. A group of his students were sitting together in a circle in his apartment, trying our hardest to tune in, and more importantly, to share what we were receiving. Directly across from me was a young woman who attended our class, but whom I hadn't gotten to know at that point. She was young and pretty, and I was aware of a spirit boy of about seven years old leaning against her knee. My conscious mind was telling me that there was no way a woman this young could have a seven year old child, and besides, I was so nervous waiting for my turn to speak that I could barely hang on to my impression. Stephen allowed those who were most confident to share their impressions first, and then he gently asked the rest of us to open up. And, as we students had already learned from Stephen, "I don't get anything" is not an acceptable answer!

I think I was the last to speak up and volunteer my impression of this boy. It took me several minutes to gather the confidence to say that I saw him. During this agonizing silence (when I was certain everyone was rolling their eyes), I was aware that the boy came over and stood directly in front of me. When he was sure that I had his attention, he turned and walked back to stand by the young woman across from me. Finally I said it.

"I see a boy of about seven or eight by Kathy," I whispered. "He's leaning on her knee." Then, to my astonishment and delight, Stephen said he was aware of him, too. Kathy then acknowledged that her son's playmate had an older brother in spirit. If it weren't for the patience of my teacher and the persistence of this spirit boy, I probably wouldn't have said anything.

These days I offer regular open circles at a local healing arts center, and on one evening I had a group of nine women in attendance. The first spirit person to come through was a boy of two or three years old, who was showing me he'd passed in what looked like a car seat. The woman I was directing him to, denied knowing a small child who had passed. As she said to me after I continued to press this little boy on her, "I think I'd remember a tragedy like *that* in my family!" Another woman seated right beside me offered to claim this spirit boy, when she explained that an adolescent in her family died. He wasn't in a car seat, but rather confined to some sort of special bed with a kind of harness. I tuned in to this information (normally I ask my guests not to offer this much detail, but she'd managed to get it all out before I could stop her), and became aware of this other spirit person. But the little guy I'd originally brought in wasn't going to be dropped so easily! He practically shrieked at me, as only toddlers can, to get my attention. He was tugging my hand and energetically dragging me over to the first woman I'd addressed.

"Okay, okay!" I said to him, as I turned to the first woman once again. She was already shaking her head. "He passed in a car seat, he's showing me a neighborhood driveway..."

"Wait! Now I know!" she shouted, before I'd finished my sentence. "When you said the word 'neighborhood' I remembered!" A neighbor had been in a car accident in which her young child—in a car seat—had been killed. As it turns out, my guest was planning to meet with this young mother in the near future. That little boy was going to kick and scream till he got his message through, that he was quite alive and well, and aware of his physical family.

One family drove quite a distance to come see me for a circle a few years ago. A spirit girl came through for one of the daughters, showing me a violent impact. She came through saying she was a peer, what the spirit people say to me when they mean that they are not old enough to be a parent, nor young enough to be a child, of the guest. She referred to a wedding that she attended in spirit.

My guest acknowledge that her friend had perished when she was hit by a train, and that a mutual friend had married since that tragedy. The bride had planned to ask this spirit girl, before she died, to be a bridesmaid. With our connection complete, I thanked the spirit person. Just as I was preparing to move on, the spirit girl pulled my attention over to a cousin who, it turns out, was also quite well acquainted with the spirit girl.

"Did you make fun of her nose when she was in the casket?" I asked, incredulous. "Because she shows me that she saw you standing around her, making fun of the way her nose was rebuilt."

When the shrieks of laughter died down, the cousin explained. She said that they had all, but she principally, remarked on what a poor job the undertaker had done recreating the spirit girl's face after the accident.

I told them their friend in spirit was having fun with them. "She says, 'I'm lying here in a casket, and all you can talk about is how my nose looks?!'—but she's laughing hysterically. She really gives me the feeling that she's the life of the party, and would be the first to laugh at a good joke, even about herself."

"That's definitely her," they all nodded in agreement. Everyone there felt as though this refreshing spirit person was truly in their midst, with her own humor and personality.

CHAPTER 15

Suicide

In 2010, I organized a psychic fair in my small town. Throughout the day, visitors could partake of many different sorts of readings, from tarot to palm to animal and spirit communication. In the evening I offered a free open circle, which was attended by over fifty people— some of whom had come with friends, but most of whom had never met each other.

As I began to bring in the spirit people, I could tell right away it was going to be challenging with such a large group sitting in a circle. I read for about twenty minutes, and then was pulled to one small cluster of people.

"I feel like I have a young person here, I feel like he was a male, but maybe confused about being a male, or maybe wasn't yet a full grown male. He tells me he made a mistake. He should have spoken and he didn't speak, he shows me his hand over his mouth. Something kept him from speaking or saying something about himself, and so he didn't, and as a result of that he passed away. I don't feel like there was a crime, but I feel like people felt it was a crime in a way. 'Oh, this is such a shame, it's almost a crime'—that people would say something like that. In a sense he's taking responsibility, that he needed something and he didn't ask for it. He needed to say something and he didn't say it, and he felt he wouldn't have another chance, so he's taking responsibility for a choice he made, that he had a hand in his passing. His actions led to his own passing. He wants to say 'if I had only said something, this "crime" wouldn't have happened.'"

Six people who didn't know each other, but who were all seated in the same area, raised their hands to acknowledge this spirit. It turns out there were several young males in spirit whose actions had lead to their passing. All were under the age of twenty. We determined that one was confused about his gender identity and didn't know how to express it; another had passed away during the commission of a petty crime; the family of another had to listen to friends and relatives say what a "crime" it was that their son had killed himself, that he wouldn't be in heaven; yet another suffered from a mental illness. There wasn't one other guest with a suicide to acknowledge in the *entire crowd*. Somehow these strangers had all been guided to sit in the same area.

"I couldn't have seated you all here together if I'd wanted to!" I said, and after a couple of unique details were attributed to certain spirit people by certain guests, the time had come to speak for all of them.

"The primary message that comes through is what the crime was, if you can call it a crime, is that these young men made decisions that led to their passing. I feel like they're saying that the transition was seamless. If they had recovered their senses, so to speak, while they were still in the physical, they would have become the men that they are now, in the spiritual world. So even though life in the physical body ended, growing continued, maturing continued, and spiritual evolution continued. They fully acknowledge that they made a choice. At least one of them saw an opportunity to say 'I need help' or 'I'm going to take my own life.' Let me leave this message from all of them: If there was some talk here in the physical that, 'Oh, they won't go to heaven,' or 'If you take your own life, or do drugs ...' that's bullshit. They're all telling me they're where they're supposed to be, in the light and love of their heavenly parent, and they're maturing and growing up where they are. And that they recognize that there was a different choice that they could have made."

I was truly astonished that six different family groups with a similar kind of loss sat in the same area. It's hard to believe that their spirit people didn't have something to do with that arrangement. The message from all of them, coming through with one voice, was that they had not condemned themselves to hell by taking their own lives. They certainly weren't condoning it, as each one acknowledged he could have made different choices—but having made the choice they did, they continued to grow and learn.

It defies human compassion when I hear my clients with suicide in the family, tell me that other relatives or friends have judged their loved ones so harshly. Think about it! You're grieving the loss of a loved one, battling the guilt and bewildering emotions that accompany a suicide, and along comes some self-righteous know-it-all to add to your suffering by telling you your loved one is burning in hell! That really gets me going, and may be why spirit people who have committed suicide come through so strongly with this very same message.

I've noticed that the language of suicide has different shades, depending upon the degree of responsibility a spirit acknowledges. A soldier returning from Iraq who jumped off the Tappan Zee bridge said, "I took my own life." A young man who got behind the wheel after having too much to drink said, "my actions led to my passing." A woman in spirit who spent a lifetime indulging bad habits, only to pass from diabetes complications claimed, "I let myself deteriorate, and that's why I passed." One youngster who was involved with drugs and died of an overdose told us, "I made a series of bad decisions." A retired sailor who drank himself to death over many decades said, "I let myself spiral down and didn't stop myself." The young man mentioned in Chapter 9, who died after trying heroin for the first time said, "I made one big mistake." Each of these spirit people acknowledge that their actions led to their passing, and yet they all come through from a place of awareness, love, and spiritual well-being. Not a single one of them reports being punished. Remember that, once in spirit, we are no longer bound by our judgmental natures and human ego. Everything about life here on the physical plane is seen with much more clarity.

The spirit people who've taken their own lives are still very sensitive to the mess they've left behind, as our group of young men talked about at the psychic fair message circle. They're aware that physical people may be judging them, and that they've created a deep wound in the family they've left behind. At one circle, a spirit person came in who showed me that he was an award-winning wrestler, and was acknowledged as a guest's brother. The wrestler mumbled that he'd been responsible for his own passing, though he caused me to trip over my own words, assuring those present that, "it wasn't out and out suicide." When he showed me his medals around his neck, I felt as if I were choking on them. I continued to deliver this very mixed message of suicide/not suicide, and made sure to deliver the message that he was in the company of parents and a sister. My guest, his brother, seemed happy to hear from him.

Several days later I received an e-mail from that guest's wife. She said the wrestler brother had indeed committed suicide by hanging himself, but that the family, devout Irish Catholics, didn't talk about it or admit it was suicide. This spirit person was concerned that the real message—that he was in heaven with loved ones—would be missed, if too much focus was placed on the fact of his suicide. He gave me information that his brother could hear, but also information that his sister-in-law could pick up on without distressing the brother. She ended her e-mail by saying her husband hadn't slept so well in years since attending our circle, and hearing that his brother was at peace.

As I've mentioned in previous chapters, many a spirit person has claimed responsibility for taking his own life, and not one of them was reporting from the fiery environs of hell. When you hear about suicide, or if you are unfortunate enough to lose a loved one to suicide, try to refrain from making judgments. Be compassionate. Even these devastating choices and their consequences will make sense when we rejoin our loved ones in the spirit world. And if you're contemplating taking your own life, be assured that you will not be escaping your challenges by making such a choice. Your challenges still await you in the spirit world, where you will continue to grow, learn, and evolve. Why not try again to stay here and work them out, if for no other reason than to spare your family pain. I remember a client whose mother took her own life, and whose father, so lost without his wife, followed by his own hand a few months later. My client to this day grapples with this tragedy.

CHAPTER 16

How The Spirit Goes Out

Last week I sat for a few minutes of meditation. One of my guides I call The Gentleman (who shows himself as a skeleton) came in after a few minutes. I asked him to show me what happens after a spirit leaves a body, and he showed me that the spirit goes into a deep sleep. When I asked him for how long, he just shrugged. *It depends on the time they need to adjust,* he answered. He showed me that while the spirit person is in this deep sleep, something like a scan passes over them. It looked like what I've seen on TV of a radar line sweeping around a dial, detecting bumps and blips with little flares of light.

The Gentleman showed me the scan going back and forth until all blips and flares of light were gone, revealing just a line moving uninterrupted over the spirit person. *Is it cleaning? Resetting energy?* I asked him in my mind, but he didn't answer me. He kind of clacked his teeth together when I asked, and of course it always looks like he's smiling, so I got no further with this line of inquiry.

Many famous psychic mediums write or speak about exactly what happens when we die. But how can any living person know something like this exactly? How can an experience that is so beyond our conscious ability to process, be given to us to understand? So, in answer to my question, I feel like my guide gave me a facsimile of something that could happen, but any further information wouldn't be comprehensible to me. In the hundreds of past life regressions that I've conducted, I always ask my clients what happens after they die in a former life. Most report their spirit coming out through the mouth, head, or chest of the body they're vacating. Beyond that none have been able to say. Even in my own meditations and regressions, I have gotten to that point and then been led to focus on something else. We may know, anecdotally of course, how the spirit leaves the body, but I believe we can't know what happens next with any certainty. Not as long as we're living here with our conscious, rational minds for company.

Yet "what happens next" is a very important piece of information that living people are hungry for, if not for their own future in the spirit world, than for reassurance that their loved ones are okay. Therefore, it's a key piece of information I ask the spirit people for when they come through. "How did you pass away and what did you suffer from before dying?" I ask them to show me something a loved one did for them after they passed, so my clients will know that, at least immediately after death, their loved ones were aware of them. I also stress to my clients before every reading or message circle that by no means are their spirit people still suffering from these diseases or injuries. They are simply bringing them forward as an identifying characteristic.

Alzheimer's Disease or Dementia

Few things are more heart-wrenching than watching a beloved parent or grandparent slowly forget their habits, their lives, and their families. Many times in the course of private readings or message circles, a spirit person has come through giving me the feeling of mental confusion, isolation, depression, and an inability to communicate. These spirit people recall watching their family try desperately to connect with them, and some have seen their family members stay away entirely, because they're so distressed. One elderly spirit person showed herself sitting in a chair in some sort of residential facility, where she was parked in her wheelchair, and left alone for much of the day.

The messages those spirit people most often pass on is to free oneself of guilt. A client of mine whose father passed away in a nursing home in Florida, found that message so incredible she asked me to repeat it again and again. She'd avoided going to see him for years, because she couldn't bear that her dad didn't recognize her. In order to ensure that I was reporting directly what her father said to her, I asked him to give me something very specific about their connection. Anything to help her move on in her life, without feeling she'd abandoned or rejected him.

"You're not going to believe this," I said to my client. To her father in spirit I said, "Do I really have to say this?"

"Say what?" she asked me.

"Um, okay. Really? Okay, uh, your father—no, I'm not going to do it—wants me to sing the Hokey Pokey song. I told him I'd tell you that he said it, but that I'm not going to sing it." I said.

"Oh my God! He always sang that to me, we always did that dance when I was little, and even when I was growing up we'd joke around with that song!" My client was laughing and crying at the same time (a pretty common condition at readings).

"Well, he's singing it and doing the Hokey Pokey right now," I said. "He says that before he went out he did the Hokey Pokey with the spirit world. He's singing, 'I put my left hand in, I took my left hand out ...' and he means to say he took time to venture into the spirit world in parts, until he felt comfortable going there fully." This spirit man went on to say that he would spend increasingly longer periods of time in the spirit world, though his body was still in a facility in Florida. He assured his daughter, my client, that she had no reason to feel guilty. As he said, "I wasn't really there." She left our session feeling greatly relieved and happy that her dad had come through with such a personal, meaningful story to illustrate his transition.

Other spirit people who have suffered from Alzheimer's Disease or advanced states of dementia report very similar types of transitions. More than one has come through acknowledging their loved ones' distress, as they tried to reach them through their mental fog at the very end. Nearly every one has said something like "you couldn't reach me, because I wasn't there." Some have been more specific, and gone on to describe understanding what was being said to them by their visiting families, but not having the ability to get that understanding into a place in their brains where they could process a response.

If you have a loved one enduring this disease now, just know that their transition is usually gradual, comfortable, totally under their spiritual control. They are aware of your visits, words, and touch ,even if they are unable to respond coherently. And above all, forgive yourself if you've lost a loved one to this disease and felt you didn't visit or do enough. Once our people go out to the spirit world they don't hold grudges!

Cancer and Other Diseases

When a spirit person comes through having passed from cancer, they always show me the image that's become symbolic for, at least, breast cancer: the graphic of a ribbon crossed over itself. A spirit person will show me the cancer ribbon over the liver, stomach, breast, brain, or whatever other organ or body part that was the most affected. If a person's cancer moved from one place to another, or appeared in one place, went into remission, and then cropped up somewhere else, the spirit people show me a cancer ribbon on it's side. For instance, I may see the organ of a uterus with a sideways cancer ribbon floating over it, and simultaneously feel a pain in my chest. I would say to my client, "Cancer began in the uterus and moved to the breast, or began in the breast and reappeared in the uterus." For identification, they may show me terrible pain or unquenchable thirst, or give me a feeling that I'm very heavily medicated.

When a spirit wants to talk about something like hereditary heart disease, they'll give me the feeling of squeezing in my heart while showing me a DNA spiral. The DNA spiral has become symbolic for me of any disease that was passed down to the person in spirit, or which the person in spirit has passed down to one of their children still living. In messages like this, the spirit person may remind their loved one here in the physical world to "keep an eye on this." They don't see the future, they don't know our fate, but they know that their physical family members may have inherited something from them, and they want them not to ignore it. Sometimes the spirit people will show me the DNA spiral when they're talking to their descendants about more minor conditions, like bad teeth, difficulty conceiving, or migraine headaches, as they mean to say "you have the same problem I did." I'll also get the DNA spiral when the spirit person is referring to a talent, such as athletic ability or musical gifts. They're proudly saying "you get it from me."

Leukemia, tuberculosis, diabetes, and diseases of the blood make me feel as though I'm sick at my very core, completely weak and fatigued, and giving messages from spirit people who passed with these conditions is often difficult at first. But, as with every message, once the spirit is identified and acknowledged the clairsentient impression of weakness or pain disappears. Spirit people who suffered from advanced cases of diabetes share with me their neuropathy, their amputations, and their comas. Many spirit people plagued with these illnesses talk about their physical struggles and their mental exhaustion, and, as a healthy person, I've learned much more patience and compassion than I might have otherwise.

When it takes a long time to pass away into the spirit world, or if a person battles cancer or any other chronic illness, it's almost impossible to understand the depth of their courage and fortitude from a place of wellness. Even a moment of the impression of a debilitating disease is enough for me. I can't wait to get that spirit acknowledged, so that terrible feeling can go away. It comes as no surprise therefore, that many spirit people who pass from long drawn out illnesses practically leap for joy when released from their physical bodies into the spirit world. As hard as it may be to lose these loved ones, it would do those of us left behind a world of good to celebrate their freedom with them.

A young woman came to see me whose uncle had passed from ALS, commonly known as Lou Gehrig's Disease. No cure exists for this terrible illness, which renders the body immobile, while the mind stays sharp. People who suffer from ALS lose the ability to walk, to talk, to swallow, and finally to breathe on their own—all while fully aware of their diminishing physical capacities. My client adored her uncle and his young children, and the whole family watched with disbelief as this athletic, vibrant, handsome, young husband and father faded away before their eyes. When I brought him through and he was acknowledged, I was in tears as I attempted to convey his state of mind. The unbounded joy and freedom he gave me to feel was beyond description. Now it was my turn to laugh and cry at the same time! His message was that all that had led up to his passing was forgotten, and though he had been "trapped in his body," he was now completely liberated. He needed his family to know that he was better than he could even have imagined, now that he was in spirit.

Terminating Life Support and Giving Permission

Many long, drawn-out illnesses finally end when a member of the family elects to terminate life support, or to sign papers asking the medical staff not to resuscitate or extend heroic measures of care to an ailing loved one. Quite a few of these decisions are actually made with the advance approval of the patient, yet my clients still carry a huge burden of grief or regret for having made the decision that released their beloved family member to the spirit world.

When I bring through a spirit person who was on life support before passing, he will give me the feeling that I'm not breathing on my own. My sense is that air is being pushed into my lungs, rather than naturally drawn in by the act of my lungs expanding. When I feel as though this air is being pushed into me, I know right away that the person could not breathe without support. I usually also feel that I have something that fills my mouth and throat. It's quite a claustrophobic feeling, more of a smothering sensation than one of relief. All the spirit people who have come through showing themselves on life support before passing, have urgently pressed the message on me that they are grateful that permission was given for them to go out. Every single time, in every circle, or at every reading, the spirit person has given me the claustrophobic feeling of suffocating on this breathing machine, and shouting "Thank you!" when it was finally turned off.

I once gave a message from a spirit person who was in a coma for three months before he passed away. Just like those who suffered with Alzheimer's Disease, this man told us all that he'd been out of the physical body for quite some time. When his life support was finally discontinued, he felt it was a blessing at last to be free of his non-functioning body. Knowing he would never return to his body, yet being tied to it all the same, caused this person to wish he could just be "cut loose," as he said. He witnessed his family come and chat with his "shell" while he longed to tell them to let him go and to move on. He was so happy for the opportunity to come through in spirit, to let them know they did the right thing. He had been worried that they would fixate too much on the presence of his body as evidence that he was alive, and not on his sense of self. Most of all, he wanted to let them know that he actually was still alive, still here, still part of the family, perhaps now more than while in a coma.

Sometimes permission doesn't involve something as dramatic as turning off life support machines or withholding care. My own grandfather passed away almost twenty years ago, after several long months of treatment for stomach cancer. When the cancer spread to his liver and the doctors suggested a liver transplant, he refused. He was in his seventies, he said, and available organs should go to younger people with more life ahead of them. In time, he was home with my grandmother and preparing to cross over. As he felt the time draw near, he told her she had to let him go. He said that Jesus was calling to him, but he couldn't go if she wouldn't let him. In tears my grandmother said, "Okay honey, you can go," and he passed away into the spirit world shortly thereafter. My grandfather has come to me only a couple of times since then, and when he does he's always smiling and peaceful in the way only spirit people can be.

Whether permission is given between two sweethearts or between a family member and medical staff, every single spirit person I've ever brought through has come in with "Thank you!," "Bless you!," or "You did the right thing!"

Sudden or Unexpected Death

My friend Kellie was at a message circle at my house with her sister and several others. I had a peer of hers named Monica come through saying "I was here, and then I was gone." This young woman was acknowledged by Kellie as having passed unexpectedly in her sleep. She showed me toasting with a glass of champagne and mentioned a "special niece," both of which were verified by Kellie. Apparently, on the morning of her death she was to close on refinancing her house so that she would be able to keep it following her divorce. The champagne was already in the refrigerator chilling for the toast. She had no actual nieces, but was referring to the daughter of a dear friend who lived abroad. Monica had just changed her will a few months before her passing, bequeathing everything to this young lady. One of the most interesting parts of this story is that her former husband was still the owner of record of their house—the refinancing never happened—and therefore took possession of it at Monica's death. Kellie told us that Monica had always said her ex-husband would only get the house "over my dead body."

Jill came for a private reading quite recently and showed me a picture of two young women, saying only that they were her best friends. At first I thought Jill was asking me to tune in psychically rather than for spirit communication, but that quickly cleared up. I pointed to one of the women in the picture who gave me the impression of a stunning impact to the side of my head.

"Was this a vehicle accident?" I asked. "I don't know if I have one person here or two."

"Yes," Jill answered.

"But she didn't pass right away though? Was there some time?" I felt a lingering, but it didn't seem consistent with this powerful blow to my head.

"No, she died instantly," Jill said. "The other girl died three months later. There was a three month gap between them, they were best friends."

I was shocked that both girls in the picture died, and I had to clarify that with Jill. I initially had gotten the feeling that I had two spirit people with me, but the presence seemed to resolve itself into one. Both of them being in spirit did explain the conflicting information I was getting.

"I don't know if I have one person here or two," I said again.

"They tend to talk over each other," Jill said. "Every medium I've ever been to can't separate them, they can't tell them apart."

Martha's husband staggered away from the table one night after dinner, suffering a massive stroke and a heart attack. While waiting for the ambulance to arrive, Martha told me she spoke to Frank continuously, though he was unable to speak to her. At the hospital he seemed to stabilize, but then began to deteriorate rapidly. He passed away around four o'clock in the morning. A few months after this completely unexpected tragedy, I was doing a reading for Martha in her home. Her greatest concern, like many of us who lose a loved one like this, was that he had suffered. Not knowing any of the details except that he had passed away from a stroke, I felt Frank come through.

"He shows me he's here in the house, but up away from his body, like he's a balloon attached to himself. When the paramedics take him out on the stretcher, he's trailing behind just like he was a helium balloon, kind of following himself out the door."

Martha wondered if he'd heard what she said.

"He tells me that he is extremely surprised. He gives me a sense of 'What the hell was *that*?' when he finds himself outside of his body. Like, 'What was that sound?' and then he's watching the whole thing happening. I feel no pain in my body, and he's saying that the groaning noises coming from his body are more like biological, not emotional. He doesn't feel pain to match the loud groaning sounds he's making. My feeling over all is one of being very cushioned both emotionally and physically. Not stuffy or insulated, just kind of like nothing has an edge. It's a very easy feeling. Surprised, but not worried."

I share these three examples of unexpected passing, to illustrate how normal it seems to the spirit people. A few of them express surprise as Frank did, saying "What the hell happened?" Most carry on in spirit communication the same way those who linger do. That is to say, everything here is as it's supposed to be.

My own dad passed quite unexpectedly at the age of sixty-four. He wasn't feeling well one day, thought he might be getting the flu, so he stayed home from work. My mother came home from her teaching job to find him dead in bed. We all assumed it was a heart attack, as he'd had a double bypass about ten years before. A medium brought him in for me a couple of years after his passing, describing his complete and utter surprise that he was now in the spirit world. The medium showed a small piece of plaque detaching from my dad's artery, moving up to his brain, and causing a stroke. He kept repeating how surprised my dad was, to find himself out of his body. Surprised, but not at all distressed. When I told my mother about this she told me she thought he looked surprised. She found him on his back in bed, and with both his arms over his head. She said he looked just like a little boy who'd been surprised.

Whether our loved ones linger, die suddenly, or even perish by their own hand, let's all remember here in the physical world that they are all peacefully, happily, and compassionately enjoying their present state. All they want us to do is to stop grieving, to recognize that they are still very much alive, still witnessing family events important and mundane, and to remember that we'll all meet again.

Mental Illness

When a person comes through who suffered from some sort of mental illness, they give me various feelings and symbols to convey their condition. A schizophrenic man came through and showed me that his mind was split in two, with the halves not meeting together in the right place. A deeply depressed person gives me a terrible sinking feeling, as though my emotions and good feeling plummet, and at the same time shows me her face buried in her hands. At a Spiritualist Church where I sometimes conduct services, I gave this compelling message from a middle-aged man in spirit. He'd had a mental handicap such as Down's Syndrome or autism:

"He gives me the feeling of being an adult, but not being an adult at the same time. Not because he's shirking his responsibilities, but because he can't care for himself or hold a job," I said.

"He's talking about someone who has a young person, a brother or sister or child who has such an issue like autism, where they're socially, mentally, or emotionally not developing as what we would classify as normal. He's directing this message to people who have someone like that in their life, and to say he didn't feel—and he's speaking in general for people like himself—'we don't feel as though something is missing, we feel'—he's telling me—that he himself and 'people like me' he says, 'we are very, very close to God, and we are very close to who we are as biological organisms as well, so we have an ability to recognize the personhood that we have in a human body. We also recognize the spirits we are because this division, this cleft, is so clear, that we're in this body that's supposed to function this way, with this brain and mind and synapses that are supposed to function this way, and they don't.'

"Those of us who do function this way, who function normally, we lose sense of our spirituality and how close we are to God, and he says those like himself do not. 'There's nothing about us to feel sorry for, or to feel pity for, rather there's something to envy, because we still very much recognize the two parts that make up the whole person we are when we come into this world as human beings, with personalities and egos. We see the distinction between those things,' he says, 'so we can see the largeness of ourselves who come down into the smallness of a person.'"

A woman in the congregation raised her hand when I was finished with this very descriptive message, knowing it was for her sister's two children who are autistic. This amazing spirit went on with quite a sense of humor as he continued his efforts to get me to convey his message with accuracy.

"I want to get this right, he's making me laugh, saying, 'what are you, stupid?' and thumping me on the head. He's giving me this complex feeling and idea that I'm trying to get into the 'little person' of my own mind and now I see, he's giving me the difference of how that feels, and it's really very unique how I have to take this huge understanding and then pass it through the filter of the vocabulary I have and my tongue and lips and teeth, and it's not really working."

I still haven't really found the words to describe the clairsentient feeling this spirit person gave me. While alive in his physical body, he was for all intents and purposes unable to care for himself, yet at the same time more alive and vast in his mind and self-awareness than I could even grasp. Taking that awareness and trying to make it fit in a personality and so-called normal mindset was impossible—but that didn't mean he was a person to pity. He had an awareness of his holiness and perfection of spirit that he simply couldn't translate in the physical world. Maybe the rest of us are blissfully ignorant of our own perfection and hugeness of spirit, and so we are able to fit in with the society we've created. I don't have any more information than what this spirit person shared about mental illness, but I know when I go out into the spirit world this message will make perfect sense.

Murder

Only a handful of spirit people have come through declaring that they were murdered. Most of them concerned young men whose "actions led to their passing," because they were dealing drugs or involved in other crimes. At one message circle, I was reading for a guest named

Carmen when I became aware of the presence of a couple of young men in spirit, who'd died violently.

"I see a man laid out on a slab. I feel like this person died violently, either had a head injury or hit his head really badly on the ground. Do you know someone who was murdered? Or who died really violently? I see someone laying on his back and there is all this trauma around the head. I'm hearing the world 'killed.'

"I have a couple of cousins who died in car accidents."

"With a bad head injury?" I asked her.

"Yes," was Carmen's reply.

"Okay. At least one of them, the one who is here, isn't taking responsibility. That means that he's telling me in a sense it wasn't his fault. That's why he was saying 'I was killed,' because they'll own up to it if it was their fault. But he's giving me the feeling that it just happened. Do you know the circumstances of these car accidents?" I asked her.

"A truck hit them, his brother was driving."

"The other one I'm seeing feels to me that he is broad, well-formed, not skinny or lanky. He's saying 'I was killed." Something happened where he was killed. Do you have someone who was murdered? He *is* taking responsibility. Also a tremendous amount of trauma or blood around the head." The spirit was showing me that he was bragging about selling drugs, and that he got in over his head. For him it was fun, but for his bosses it was business. Because he was talking too much, he was executed. "Was he involved in something that wasn't necessarily on the up-and-up?" I asked her.

"Yes!" Carmen was surprised that this came through, though she said the family suspected he was involved in crime.

"He's saying he was murdered, he'd been killed."

"Yes, that makes sense," she said.

"From where he is now there is no problem, he's coming through now with these gory details to help identify himself to you." The exact details of this man weren't known, because he'd died out of the country, and the real cause of death hadn't been shared with the family. They'd suspected he'd been involved in something illegal, and when they'd gotten news of his death they'd all agreed it was likely because of his involvement in something criminal. Having him come through with this information confirmed their ideas about his lifestyle and death, and allowed them some closure.

Brenda came to me a couple of years ago for a private reading. Her brother came in right away.

"A young man comes in talking about being a dad. I feel like there is male spirit here who's showing me a medal around his neck, like someone would win in sports. He's also showing me there is an older man who is still here, who is weeping." The spirit man was showing me an image of what looked like a grandfather crying, but he was giving me the feeling of a father.

"That's my father," Brenda said. She recognized her athletic brother in spirit, and that her brother was referring to their father.

"But he's much older," I said. "Is your father an older father?"

"Yes, he's in his eighties now," she answered.

"He's reaching out and wanting to say 'I recognize there is grief in this person.' He's connecting with your father in this way. This young male spirit gives me a feeling of having a very difficult time breathing, as though he is being given oxygen. Is this your brother?" I asked

"Yes, that's Jimmy." I went on to give more detail about Brenda's brother Jimmy, which she validated. Our reading continued with the usual kind of funny and mundane messages that the spirit people often share, to assure their loved ones that they're still part of the family. Then, without warning, I felt that I was on drugs or medication. Brenda confirmed that this, too, was connected to Jimmy. Her brother then spoke a little about his son, and asked that Brenda care for him as much as possible. He described a tense, unstable relationship with the child's mother, Maria, one that Jimmy had stayed in despite a lot of drama. He gave a message that he was intending to leave the relationship before he passed away—all of which Brenda confirmed. He then gave a rather strange message to Brenda. Referring to Maria, he said that "she had nothing to do with it."

We continued for approximately forty-five minutes, bringing in other friends and family members. We were nearing the end of our reading when Brenda brought up her brother Jimmy once again.

"Could you please ask Jimmy to tell me if Maria poisoned him," she asked me.

"No, I don't get the feeling that she had a hand in his passing. He came through earlier and said that she had nothing to do with it. They might have been really butting heads, but that she wasn't responsible for his passing. He comes right back in with a 'No.' Was he autopsied?" I asked.

Brenda nodded.

"And they found poison in him?" I asked her.

"No. But when I asked for the autopsy, I told the medical examiner the situation, and she said it was messy, that I needed a lawyer, and that they were just going to do a general autopsy with the toxicology. But she wouldn't check for specific things."

"Okay," I continued. "When he came in earlier, he came in telling me that she had nothing to do with his passing. When you asked, specifically, he came right in with a 'No.' For all her instability and craziness, he says there isn't maliciousness in her craziness. Just instability there, that's the impression he's giving me about her."

"I could see Jimmy saying something like that," she replied.

"But you disagree?" I asked.

"Oh yeah," she said. "Because of the boy. He's protecting her because of the boy."

"Well, if you recognize that your brother would do or say certain things, than take his message that she wasn't responsible with a grain of salt, though he gave me a very strong 'No,' very quickly."

"That's the way he was," Brenda answered. "I'm not surprised."

"It's your decision, but he was very quick to deny," I responded.

"Was he ever suspicious?" she asked.

"He gives me the impression that he went along with Maria's worldview. She is able to, because of the drama or the level of energy in the way she communicated, that he bought into it. He went along with it for a long time, but towards the end he was saying 'Enough, no.'"

"I'm not surprised. They didn't really have a life together, like you said, but to keep the peace he went along with her, and thought of her as 'not well.'"

"Well," I said, "he's giving me the impression that there was nothing malicious in what she was doing, just instability. You know him better than I do, I'm just meeting him for the first time, so by all means if you feel in your gut that there is something to go further with, don't let his words coming through me stop you. But he was very quick to say 'No.'"

Brenda was convinced that her brother was murdered by his wife, and even though the message I brought through didn't confirm her suspicions, she still felt that there was foul play. Brenda suspected her brother was still acting as he would have were he alive, denying something so as not to upset the other family members. Whether or not this is true, I have no idea. I simply passed on the message I got from Jimmy, and as any ethical psychic medium should do, I avoided giving advice, and left all decision-making to the client. If the client needs to pursue legal action or inquire more deeply into the death of a loved one, they are within their rights. I would never presume to encourage or discourage them.

More Unusual Exits

I was leading an open message circle to more than a dozen women, when I got the feeling of a late middle-aged man in spirit. He came in leading with his enormous erection, and impressed on me a kind of boastfulness about his personality. This guy was a real man's man, and kept butting in while I was working with other spirit people. I asked him (in my mind), to give me a different detail to offer, but he just floated the image of his erection right in front of me. With a sigh, I turned to a woman seated about one-third of the way around the circle.

"I have a male coming in showing me his erection and boasting about his manhood, I'm sorry to say," I announced. Lots of laughter followed, as I expected.

"He's boasting about his skill with the ladies, and he gives me the feeling of being kind of crude, or lewd, in his 'appreciation' of women." No one spoke up to claim this character, so I asked him for something, please, other than his genitals, which no one present recognized.

"He says he isn't your relative, but almost. He is short, stocky, and has tattoos on his arms. He's a smoker. He is saying the name

Laura or Laurie. He's showing me his erection because he says he died having sex."

With a shout of laughter, the woman I had been trying to bring this man to acknowledged knowing him. He was the father of her very good friend Laurie, and he had indeed passed away while having sex years ago, when the two friends were teenagers. We all got a good laugh out of that, though I was blushing fiercely during the entire exchange!

At another circle I brought through a spirit man who at first couldn't be claimed. I kept bringing him to a young woman on my right, though she was unable to identify him. When I asked him for more detail, the spirit showed me that he had passed from a violent impact, and that he had gone to school with the woman's husband. Recognition began to dawn on my guest, but true acknowledgement came when the spirit man, named Ron, showed me that he had a dog with him.

"He's saying the dog passed with him, or that they went out together," I said, which brought the following answer from my astonished guest: "His dog was stuck on the train tracks, and they were both killed by a train while he was trying to get him loose."

Ron came through to get a message of greeting to my guest's husband, and to let them know he was alright. In the company of his dog, he was cheerful and comfortable.

I have brought through several other spirit people who passed in unusual ways, but these two stand out for me because of one's crazy humor and the devotion of another for his dog.

A Note About Animal Companions

I have heard so many poignant messages from spirit people who have come through with their animal companions. Horses, parrots, cats, and dogs have not only made their distinctive presence known in readings or circles, but on more than one occasion have been the ones to first meet the person when he or she goes out of their human body and into the spirit world. I even had the pleasure of bringing in an iguana!

Sometimes the animals come in on their own, particularly if they were connected to a guest more so than a spirit person who has passed. Cats will usually go sit right next to their person and wait to be noticed. Dogs will usually stick their snouts right up in my face, so I can see right up their nostrils, and then go back and forth between me and their person. One dog even identified himself by giving me the impression of a really ripe odor. When I asked my guest if she had a dog in spirit who had been particularly smelly, she laughed out loud and described a little Lhasa Apso that farted all the time!

In the last two message circles I conducted, pet dogs came through quite strongly. In the first one, my guest Paul's uncle came through with plenty of details to confirm his identity. The spirit uncle insisted that his dog was with him too, but Paul was unable to validate this. As I was preparing this book to go to press, I received this e-mail from Paul:

> *"I never bothered to ask my cousin if his father, my uncle (who came through that night) had had a dog named 'Teddy...' a name you repeated many times, saying that my uncle wanted my sister and I to tell the family that he is with Teddy. I finally did ask and he confirmed. Incredible."*

In the more recent circle I conducted, the host's Shitzu, Yodel, remained in the room with us the entire evening. Before closing I became aware of a small, light-colored dog in spirit, who'd been laying beside Yodel. When I noticed him he came over to me, then went to sit beside the host. She acknowledged a small dog she'd had several years ago. Another guest in the circle also claimed a dog in spirit. Then the spirit dog trotted over to sit beside yet a third guest, Nina, and made a very strong connection with me. He gave me the impression that he had returned to her.

"Do you have the feeling that your current dog is the reincarnation of a dog you've had before?" I asked Nina.

"Oh, yes!" she said. "Jake is exactly like a dog I used to have."

"Well, he's telling you that it is him, he's back with you now," I replied, "that it's his spirit in this dog you have now."

The next thing I knew, I was thinking about a Warner Brothers cartoon character called the Tasmanian Devil. I know when an impression pops into my head, totally unrelated to whatever it is I'm thinking about, that I'm receiving information from a spirit.

"Was your dog like the Tasmanian Devil?" I asked her, "because I'm seeing this cartoon character now."

"That's what I call the dog I have now. He's gone through four living room sets!" Nina answered.

"Well, your guy in spirit is acknowledging that and letting you know he came back to be with you," I said. "He's telling me that the dog spirits recycle, come back into different bodies. They like to stay connected to the people they loved." All of us in the circle were delighted to hear this message. If you've ever loved and lost an animal companion, be reassured that you will meet again in spirit, if not again in this lifetime.

I know from my own experience that it isn't only dogs who return to us in different bodies, either. Many years ago, I allowed a colleague to practice a regression technique on me, and recalled an incident at four years old. Though I'd never consciously accessed these memories, my mother had told me a story of wandering away from the yard when I was a little girl. She told me I'd followed a kitten to a neighbor's house, where an elderly woman took me inside and gave me cookies. I'd gotten quite a scolding for leaving the yard. During the regression, I was able to recall this incident with startling clarity. With a child's eyes, I saw the small gray kitten and began to follow him. He let me get closer and closer, and I recalled squatting down to pet him.

Suddenly I knew on a conscious level that I recognized this cat. I shouted happily to my colleague, "That's Lucie! That's the cat I have now!" This little kitten, who had gotten me in trouble so long ago, had come back as a dear pet who still lives with me. When I listen back to the recording of this session it makes me smile every time.

Growing up with cats and dogs, riding horses, rescuing baby birds and rabbits, I have personally connected with animals my whole life. During my troubled adolescence, I swear the only creatures that understood my angst were our family's Irish Setter and our cat. I spent hours hugging them, talking to them, and pouring out my heart, as I traveled the emotional roller coaster of my teenage years. As an adult I've been blessed to share my home with horses, sheep, dogs, cats, ferrets, and ducks.

The first time I became aware of the eternal nature of the deep bond between humans and animals, came during a message circle

I conducted many years ago. I was still getting my feet wet as a professional medium, but I'd already met spirit people of all sorts, who had perished in all kinds of ways. I felt there wasn't really anything I couldn't handle.

Directly across from me sat a woman who'd come to our open circle alone. I felt the presence of an older woman come through for her, and as I began to describe her, my guest quickly acknowledged the spirit as her grandmother.

"Do you understand the name Flora or Florence?" I asked.

With tears flowing, my guest nodded. "Yes, that's her name, Flora."

"Did you pick out the dress she was waked in? Because she says thank you for choosing the dress."

"Yes. Did I choose the right one? Because there were two that she always wore," my guest asked.

"She says she liked the blue one better, the one with the small flowers on it. Was that the one you decided on?" I asked.

"Yes," she said, "though my sister thought she'd like the other one."

"She likes the one you chose," I replied. Soon another image began forming. I waited while the spirit grandmother painted a picture in my mind's eye of isolation, deep loneliness, and grief. Can this be the same cheerful lady who came in liking her burial dress, I thought? I waited a little bit more as the picture continued to develop.

"Flora tells me a story of a terrible grief, a sense of real loneliness and mourning. She gives me the feeling that she was all alone in the last days of her life, and all alone when she died. So she was literally alone, or she felt very much alone."

My guest acknowledged that the family was scattered, and that none of the descendants lived near the grandmother. In fact, it was a couple of days before the old lady was discovered dead, and then another few days to track down the family. I waited for more from Flora while her granddaughter validated this information. Suddenly I was filled with such a profound sense of love, joy, and reunion that I could hardly speak.

"Flora shows me a dog, a light-colored or white dog, that is lean and kind of tall. Could be like a greyhound kind of dog, with very short hair and a long-ish nose. This dog comes in with her now."

"Yes, that's Queenie!" my guest exclaimed. "She loved that dog! That was her best friend and constant companion when we were little, and when the dog died Flora went into a deep depression. It was a long time before she got over it."

For the first time in my professional life, I was crying during a reading. I described how Queenie had come to Flora's side as she was passing. How the dog gently reached for Flora's hand, and guided her to where she needed to go. Flora's spirit was overjoyed to be met by her best friend. I can't begin to adequately convey the love and joy Flora gave me to feel, on being met by Queenie. Though long years had passed since they'd lived together, she trusted her dog so very much, that when she went out of her physical life and saw her dog, she knew she would follow Queenie wherever she needed to go. Flora showed me that they have been together ever since.

When I think about the dogs and cats I've lived with and loved, and consider that they may be the first to greet me when I cross over, I know that I will be without any fear, and will trustingly and peacefully follow wherever they lead me.

CHAPTER 17

Channeling Spirit Communication

As I mentioned, a medium is someone who acts as the translator from the spirit person's language to, in my case, English. A channel, or trance channel as it's sometimes called, is someone who removes herself from the message and allows the spirit to use her vocal chords to deliver the message directly.

Verbally channeling spirits is not my professional method of spirit communication, though I have practiced on occasion with colleagues or into a recorder. The messages are fascinating and cryptic, but for me the entire process leaves me feeling a little weird and uncomfortable. I much prefer to use automatic writing to channel spirit messages directly, and use this technique for reading my e-mail clients. If you're interested in exploring automatic writing, be sure to try the exercise in Chapter 19.

I recently heard from a client of mine who was feeling a little shaky about a big decision she had to make. That decision involved following her heart toward a lifestyle that meant leaving her husband. Her concern was for her husband, whether he would find passionate love, whether he would be okay when she left, and when she should initiate this difficult discussion. She was feeling a lot of fear and doubt.

I truly applaud courage in doing what the heart compels, and I can appreciate the internal struggle that precedes and follows those heart-centered decisions. I sat down at my computer to answer her, closed my eyes for a moment, and shortly became aware of a slight pressure on the back of my hands. I can type with my eyes closed, so this is an easy way for me to get my conscious mind out of the way. I began by moving my fingers on my own. They weren't being moved for me yet, I was just priming the pump with this movement. The first few words had some conscious interference, but then I found that sentences were coming through my fingers. I was totally aware of what I was writing, but it seemed like my fingers were ahead of my brain, rather than the other way around. Different than writing from my own thoughts, this felt like taking dictation. This is the message I gave to this client:

"When I do message circles or other mediumship work, the spirit people always have such a wise perspective on our struggles in life. In general they say to us, 'Trust that nothing is really as big a deal as you think it is. Trust that everyone will be okay, including yourself. This will all make sense when you're dead.' Then they fill the room up with lots of laughter and joyful energy.

"That's what letting things unfold is all about. Trust that if you feel your heart (not your head) is guiding you or directing you, and you follow it, that you will never have been wrong, or be regretful. In the meantime, everyone will be okay, and in the end, everything will make beautiful, perfect sense.

"In answer to your questions, you don't have to figure out the right time frame to talk to your husband. When your mind is made up, and your heart has had enough of vacillating, you will be ready to confidently, compassionately, share the truth. It's better to let the time present itself, than to force it to happen.

"You may feel that you're in a terrible state of a heart torn in half, but it is unwise to force this final conversation. Finally, one day, you will wake up and it will be 'the day.' Despite ultimatums and deadlines, this conversation has to bloom organically from within you, with your own perfect initiative. And while the conversation may not be easy to have, it will be easy to begin. Ignore the pressure from your thoughts or from external sources, and you will be guided to the right time.

"As for whether your husband will find passionate love, of course the answer is this: you cannot let that stop you or delay you from your own passionate life. It is none of your business how he plumbs his own feelings, or whether or not he seeks passion. You are not responsible for the richness or fullness of his life, and as long as you carry that responsibility, you will prevent him from finding out for himself, and at the same time dilute your own experience. It's a natural thing to do when you care about someone. But be assured that released from a half-passionate life, he will be free to seek out—if *he* chooses—true fulfillment.

"Talk about your fears and doubts to God, or your angels, or your beloveds in spirit. Get every terrible thought of yourself out, if you have to tear it out by the roots. How to do that? For once and for all, for the first or last time, say out loud to God every single fear you have, every decision you regret, every action you're ashamed of. Let every sorry, wretched thought come out. Only God is listening. Let Him hear your secrets, which He knows and has forgiven before you were even born. No part of you is so black or so hidden that God's light cannot shine into.

"Leave all of that there with God or your beloveds. They want you to put those burdens down now. You are here in a physical body to live fully and with the purpose that is stamped in your heart. Be cheerful when you can. Accept that you are forgiven, even in advance of the things you have not yet done."

After receiving this message from her spirit people, my client was able to feel safe about postponing her difficult discussion without guilt or harsh self-judgment. She knows now that when the time is right—if it is still right for her—the opportunity to begin the discussion will be logical, timely and obvious.

PART FIVE

Lessons in Spirit Communication

CHAPTER 18

If You Are Going For A Reading

If you've never been to a message circle or had a private reading before, keep these tips in mind for the best experience possible.

Research. Do your research, either by talking to people who've already seen that medium, or by talking to the medium herself on the phone beforehand. Different mediums work differently. Some take a very ethereal approach, including messages from angels, spirit guides, or ascended masters. If this is not your style, you're probably not going to feel satisfied with your experience. Some mediums have very strict rules about their circles, such as no one may enter or leave once the session has started, or that the guests or clients may not speak during the circle. Mediums like myself make sure to set up a very approachable, casual, fun, and interactive experience. Others prefer a tone of mystery or seriousness. I like my clients to speak up and ask questions. Others want clients to simply listen. Find a medium who matches your desired experience, and you both will feel much more satisfied with the connection.

Most mediums bring in information via two or more channels—clairsentience and clairvoyance for example. Feel free to ask the medium how the spirit people impress their messages on him. My clairaudient abilities are not as robust as my others, so when a client asks me something like, "What does he say?" or "What does his accent sound like?" I have to translate that through feeling and images, rather than actual sound.

Expect the unexpected. Manage your expectations before going into a spirit communication session, or ask the medium how she works before your reading begins. I spend about ten minutes at the beginning of a reading reminding my client to be open to whomever might come through. If a client comes to a circle wanting only to hear from Dad, and Dad and I don't connect right away, the disappointment can disrupt acknowledgement of a great uncle, childhood friend, or co-worker who maybe was less emotionally significant. If they are hoping to hear from a very significant loved one, a reunion which is sure to bring out strong emotions, that spirit person may send in someone less significant first, just to break the ice. Many of my first-time clients are nervous when we begin, and it's always been a great start to have a former neighbor, classmate, or colleague come through first. It dispels the tension, the client gets to see how it works, and everyone relaxes a little bit.

Be open to hearing from people who may not have seemed that significant to you. They may be acting as an ambassador, and they may have an insightful or important message for you.

I did a private phone reading for an elderly woman in Connecticut some time ago. She'd never had a reading before, and though she told me I had been highly recommended by friends of hers, she was extremely skeptical. She was even combative on the phone. After explaining to her how I work, I brought through a sweetheart from her younger days who had died of prostate cancer. She was able to identify him right away, but told me rather brusquely, "I have no interest in talking to *him*. I don't know why *he's* here." As it turns out, he was there as the warm-up for her husband and brother. He came through so that she could familiarize herself with the process of the reading.

Many spirit people see an opportunity to visit with the physical world and love to just stop by to say hello. I brought in the spirit of a girl who was a high school classmate of my client, Danielle. She described herself and the circumstances of her passing perfectly, yet my client failed to acknowledge her. When the spirit insisted, I continued to advocate for her presence for many long minutes. At last Danielle admitted knowing a fellow student who had died in the manner the spirit presented. I asked Danielle why she hadn't validated the spirit girl's presence earlier, and she said, "Well, I knew her, but we weren't friends or anything."

The spirit girl went on to give a message that turned out to be quite relevant for Danielle. Yet, even if she hadn't had a specific message, her presence is a great example of how active the spirit people can be when they see an opportunity to talk about the afterlife and the spirit world.

If you work in an emergency room or nursing home, inform the medium! I can't tell you how many times I've brought through spirit after spirit for a guest, only to have her deny knowing every single one of them. The first couple of times this happened was bewildering and a bit embarrassing. Finally one spirit said, "You tried to save my life." When I asked my guest if she worked in a hospital, and she affirmed that by saying she worked in intensive care, I understood why all the unidentifiable spirit people were coming through. From that moment on, if I feel a rush of unknown spirits who are connected to a guest through a facility where they passed, I set up a boundary and request that only their personal spirit people come forward. What's most moving about these experiences is how huge an impact doctors and nurses have on the dying. So many of them take an opportunity to come in and thank the physical people.

Validate what you can. May I say this again? Validate, validate, validate! If the medium has been recommended, or if you've been referred by someone you trust, don't waste a minute of your valuable session testing him or her. It really is a waste of time, and you may miss out on an opportunity to connect. Generally a medium receives an impression or two, and then needs to take a moment to understand it's meaning before translating it to the client. I can do three or four of these impressions in a row before translating. That is, I might get the impression of a gender, understand it and store it in my working memory and wipe the slate clean, get a second impression of a first name, understand it and store it in my working memory and wipe the slate clean, and get a third impression of a cause of death. At that point I might say, "I have a female in spirit, with a name like Mary or Marie, who shows me she passed from leukemia." If you know who this lady is, please say so! When you do, it allows me to discard these three impressions I've been holding, and go back for more details. Believe me, we mediums want to convey the presence of your loved one in all the detail we can. We want you to make a connection, to be certain beyond a shadow of a doubt that your loved one is still very much alive. By acknowledging that a certain spirit may be here for you, you're only making it easier for the medium to bring through more evidence of that spirit person. If a client is testing me and has decided beforehand that they need to hear ten solid details from me before they'll validate, I may give up after translating six, thinking I'm on the wrong path. Validating doesn't mean you're giving the medium information she is supposed to be telling you. Ethical mediums won't fish for information, and will stop a client if they're giving too much. If I hear a client start to fill in too much detail when they're validating, I stop them in their tracks and say, "Let me tell *you* how this spirit person passed."

Ask for your loved ones. Though I haven't done any official record-keeping on this, I can say comfortably that when most clients thought of, or asked for the presence of, a certain spirit person before coming to a reading or circle, that spirit has come through. I once had a guest named Mary Jean attend an open circle. She had strong and clear communications from multiple spirit people. I sensed that some of the other guests were getting a bit annoyed as she sang out "That's for me!" every time I started to describe the presence of a spirit person. After the circle, Mary Jean said she had been meditating every day on four or five spirit people, though she hadn't actually committed to coming to our circle till the last minute. In fact, I'd been expecting nine guests, and ten arrived.

Mary Jean said, "I had been asking and asking for my people to come through to me, somehow. Every day in meditation, I'd been reaching out to them, and asking for them to make themselves known to me. This morning I heard about this message circle, I signed up, and I said Grandma, all you guys, I'm going to this séance tonight, and if it's really you, please show me."

Every single one of her people came through, with details that convinced Mary Jean her spirit people heard and answered her.

While this hasn't been true on every occasion, and people who never meditate still do hear from their loved ones in spirit, most clients who do request the presence of a spirit are answered by that spirit. It seems to underscore that our spirit people are still participating in our lives. If you're going to a message circle or a reading, and you know you want to hear from someone, ask them in prayer or meditation for a few days leading up to your appointment.

Be a healthy skeptic. Unfortunately, there are plenty of unethical practitioners of all sorts out there, in every field. Get a recommendation from a friend or someone else you trust, or don't be shy about calling before an appointment to determine the medium's way of working. If you sense the medium is fishing for information, either beforehand on the phone or during the reading, gently say something like "I'm not sure." Mediums will ask questions, but they should most often be for the affirmation of something a spirit person has said. For instance, I recently asked a guest, "Did you just get a new refrigerator?" because her father in spirit, who she'd already identified, was showing me that she had. When she affirmed this, she was delighted to know that her father was still participating in family events, no matter how mundane. If a medium asks for information about a loved one in spirit before you've already validated his presence, then he may be fishing for information. I have asked for clarification from my guests, but it has always been after the guest has concretely identified the spirit person. Trust your own instincts. If the message or the description of the spirit person sound too generic, ask for more information from the medium. In the end, if it doesn't feel like a good connection, don't make the appointment or ask to end the appointment early. An ethical medium will return your money cheerfully.

Wait a while between readings. Let some time pass between visits to the same medium. It will allow time for the messages from your spirit loved ones to come to pass, and it will give the medium time to forget the details about you and your spirit people. I recommend that clients come for spirit communication no more than twice a year, unless something urgent comes up. I have also programmed myself to forget clients the minute they walk out the door. I want to make sure I'm giving them a reading if they should return, and not pulling things from my memory. I've had clients return two or three times that I swear I've never met before! When they come to my house I introduce myself, and it's always a surprise to hear them say, "Yes, we've met. I was here last year." Yet to me they appear to be total strangers. I let all my guests know that they can expect that I'll forget their names, faces, and details immediately for two reasons:

1. Not everyone wants to be openly greeted by a psychic medium; many of my clients never tell their friends or family that they've come to see me; and,
2. I want to make sure I can read their spirit people as if I've never met them before; that means forgetting I've ever met them in the first place.

The spirit people cooperate with me on this too. I've seen one group of women probably eight times over the past few years, and I've met their husbands and family in spirit multiple times, yet each time this party comes, their loved ones come through with a different detail. I don't recognize them, but my guests do. So wait a while in between readings. Any medium worth her salt will ask you to do so anyway.

Wait several months after someone has passed before going to a medium. Many mediums, myself included, won't, or won't be able to, bring in the spirit of a person who has recently passed. This may be in part because the spirit hasn't developed the abilities, or doesn't have the energy to communicate with me. A larger part for me, personally and as a representative of my profession, is that I never want to appear improper. In my view, nothing is more improper than taking advantage of someone in grief. I recommend waiting six months after a loved one has passed before visiting a medium. Of course, spirit people who went out more recently than six months have come through, though for the most part our connections are weak or staticky, or require the help of a medium in the spirit world.

Just last week I was doing a private reading with a client, who was connected first with an uncle and then a grandfather in spirit. Halfway through our reading she asked, "Are there any female spirits coming through? My mother ... "

"Stop right there," I advised her. "Let me tell you who comes through." I wasn't in fact picking up on a female spirit at all, so I asked one of the male spirits to help me out. I began to get some very clear information that was coming through in a very weak way.

"The energy of this female spirit feels extremely weak," I told her. She affirmed that her mother had weakened substantially before dying. "I don't think it's that kind of weak," I answered her, though it certainly made sense. Spirit people give me the feelings they had before they died, and I sure was feeling weak.

"It's more than that. I'm getting this information about her through the uncle in spirit. Was this her brother?" I asked. My client confirmed they were brother and sister.

"She shows me she's offering a gift, which is a symbol that she's recently been to a family celebration, or she's about to go to one, and she's showing me a girl in a very pretty, very formal dress."

"My niece, her granddaughter, just had her Sweet Sixteen party," she said, validating the celebration and the dress.

It was taking a long time for this information to come through, and when it did it was very faint. So after a few more details came through, thanks to the uncle in spirit, I asked my client when her mother had died. The feebleness of the energy was just too peculiar. The client said that she'd passed away just a couple of months before.

"That explains everything!" I answered. And it also underscores the importance of acknowledging people that may seem insignificant in comparison or even unimportant. I relied totally on that uncle in spirit to help me bring in the mother's identity. If my client hadn't acknowledged him or had brushed him off, she may not have connected with her mother at all.

Not every medium has such a policy as mine, so it makes sense to ask, without giving away details when making your appointment. From time to time, more recently deceased spirit people have come through, and it's almost always been with the help of another spirit person. So, why not ensure a solid connection with a loved one by waiting six months or so after they've passed, to visit a medium?

CHAPTER 19

Developing Your Own Skills

If you're interested in developing your own spirit communication skills, the first thing you need to do is decide that you are capable. Don't let anyone tell you that you need special gifts. It's simply not true. All it takes is determination to communicate, patience, practice, and developing the confidence to translate your impressions. Create an honest intention to communicate with the spirit people; they're half the equation and, believe me, they will be able to tell if you're intentions are harmful or manipulative.

This chapter cannot define all the ways different psychic mediums can develop their skills. That's another book in itself, and there are many good ones out there. I will show you here how to get started and how to practice, so that you can begin to see results and develop confidence. If you'd like more interactive exercises to develop your psychic and spirit communication ability, download my e-book *"The Live & Learn Guide to Unveiling Your Psychic Powers. Never-Before-Told Secrets of a Psychic Medium,"* available on my website **www.liveandlearnguides.com**.

Which "Clair" Are You?

As I mentioned in Chapter 2, there are several channels through which the spirit people can impress their messages on the mind. These channels are called learning channels, as they define how we most easily take in and process information. For example, some people are very visual: they navigate best by looking at a map. For those who are stronger auditory learners, following spoken directions will get them from Point A to Point B more efficiently. I used to think I wasn't a very good medium, because I didn't hear what the spirit people were telling me. Some very popular books I'd read suggested listening for the spirit message, and, try as I might, I couldn't seem to hear anything! It was getting pretty demoralizing. I thought I was doing something wrong, or that I really couldn't connect with the spirits. I almost gave up on developing my mediumship, until a spirit person came in to a reading I was doing very early in my professional career. The client was asking me if I'd heard a name from the spirit she'd already acknowledged and identified through the visual details I'd given her. Internally I started to panic, and begged the spirit person, "*Please* tell me your name!"

In response the spirit person showed me the face of a celebrity—it was actually a dead celebrity, Ray Charles—and put a bright light around his last name. "Charles?" I squeaked out to my client. "Yes! That's him!" was her jubilant reply. I was feeling jubilant myself, as I'd just seemed to work out at least one way to get a spirit person's name. I stammered out a silent thanks to Charles the spirit, and decided that it was perfectly okay if I was one of those mediums who wasn't clairaudient.

So, if you don't get impressions through one particular channel, don't worry. The energy of spirit communication will take the path of least resistance, just like water. The impressions will flow in to your awareness in the easiest, most natural way for you.

If you'd like to determine your dominant learning channel right now, fill in this short checklist. It was developed to help determine learning styles, and I've modified it over the years to reflect the sixth sense learning channel. I've found it's the best first step in developing your personal spirit communication skills.

Working as quickly as possible, and without over-analyzing your responses, check off all the phrases that apply to you. Go with your first impression.

Visual Channel
___ Like to keep written records
___ Typically read billboards while driving or riding
___ Put models together correctly using written directions
___ Follow written recipes easily when cooking
___ Review for a test by writing a summary

__ Write on napkins in a restaurant
__ Can put a bicycle together from written instructions
__ Commit zip code to memory by writing it
__ Use visual images to remember names
__ Am a bookworm
__ Plan the upcoming week by making a list
__ Prefer to get a map and find my own way in a strange city
__ Prefer reading/writing games like Scrabble

Auditory Channel
__ Prefer to have someone read instructions when assembling a model
__ Review for a test by reading notes aloud or by talking with others
__ Talk aloud when working out a math problem
__ Prefer listening to a cassette over reading the same material
__ Commit zip code to memory by saying it
__ Use rhyming words to remember names
__ Plan the upcoming week by talking it through with someone
__ Prefer oral instructions from an employer
__ Like to stop for directions in a strange city
__ Prefer talking/listening games
__ Keep up on news by listening to radio
__ Able to concentrate deeply on what another person is saying
__ Use free time for talking with others

Auditory Channel
__ Like to build things
__ Use sense of touch to put a model together
__ Can distinguish items by touch when blindfolded
__ Learned touch system rapidly in typing
__ Move with music
__ Doodle and draw on any available paper
__ Am an "outdoors" person
__ Move easily; am well-coordinated
__ Like to feel texture of drapes and furniture in a room
__ Prefer movement games to games where one just sits
__ Find it fairly easy to keep fit physically
__ One of the fastest in a group to learn a physical skill
__ Use free time for physical activities

Now total up the number of checks under each heading:

_____ **Total Visual**
_____ **Total Auditory**
_____ **Total Kinesthetic**

If your highest number is in the Visual Channel column, you're predominantly clairvoyant. That means you'll get visual impressions most easily. The spirit person may show you what his face looks like, or show you the map of the state where he lived. Begin to develop this skill with your eyes closed, as it's much easier to see these very subtle pictures on the blank screen of your eyelids. This is my second strongest channel, and I still close my eyes during readings if an image is coming to me. I rely on my visual channel—my clairvoyance—to understand a spirit's name.

If your highest number is in the Auditory Channel column, you're mostly clairaudient. This is a channel that still remains quite elusive for me, though from time to time I have very strong clairaudient impressions. I used to think it was important to work hard at developing this channel, but now find I do just fine without it. My experiences with clairaudience, because they've been so infrequent, have been very distinct: the sound seems like an echo, or the sound that remains when someone has just stopped speaking. It's almost like I'm straining to hear an echo of what has just been said, or like I'm recreating the sound of the voice in my mind. You may want to study other mediums who use clairaudience to understand how sounds may make an impression.

If your highest number is in the Kinesthetic Channel column, you're mostly clairsentient. That is, you'll get the feeling of a spirit person. Awareness of their gender will just seem to pop into your head. You may feel as though you're suffering from what the spirit person had: heart trouble, stroke, depression, and so forth. You may also feel a change in temperature in the room, or feel pressure on part of your body. I have a regular client whose elderly wife comes through with a tingling on my lips, and I know she means for me to tell her husband that she kisses him.

Most of us are some combination of these channels. I am mostly clairsentient, and secondarily clairvoyant. In fact, my numbers are pretty close together.

Complete the sentence below, and begin to say it to yourself often:

I am primarily CLAIR (voyant) (sentient) (audient).

It's important to remember that psychic or spirit impressions are extremely subtle. Don't wait to see a spirit person with the clarity you get when face to face with a living person. You aren't likely to hear messages in the same way you hear a friend talk to you. And the feelings that come through clairsentience can be both subtle and strong, so it's important for you to remember that these are impressions of feelings.

Preparing For Mediumship

Now that you know how you're most likely to receive impressions, you can concentrate on looking for images, listening for sounds, or feeling sensations in your body. The next step involves distinguishing between your sixth sense and your other five senses. During a spirit communication, especially in the beginning, you'll need to focus all of your attention on what you're receiving, without being distracted by your body or your surroundings. A terrific way to develop this kind of focus is by a regular practice of meditation. Besides the obvious benefits of deep relaxation, peace of mind, and improved physical and emotional health, meditation helps to quiet the conscious, active mind. This is the part of the mind you need to quiet, in order to begin receiving impressions from spirit people. Besides meditating daily, I always sit for a few minutes in silence before each reading, to alert the spirit people to my preparations and to clear my mind of distracting thoughts.

Meditation also develops one's ability to concentrate, which many of us—myself included—find very difficult. If you're an adult in the twenty-first century, you have to contend with a job, commuting, raising children, managing a home, keeping fit, maintaining marriages and friendships, and paying bills. If that's not a recipe for distraction, I don't know what is. Meditation is good practice for staying focused on the subtle images in your sixth sense, while in a distracting environment. Here's a quick exercise that will give you a sense of your ability to concentrate:

> *Sit in a comfortable chair, and close your eyes. Take one or two deep breaths; deep breathing slows down the brain waves to the alpha or meditative state, and helps relax the body. Now, think about the number 5. Picture it if you're visual. Imagine running your fingers over it, if your kinesthetic. If you're strongest channel is auditory, imagine you can hear it. Concentrate on the number 5 for as long as you can.*

How long were you able to stay focused on the number 5? It's not as easy as it seems, is it? That's because most of us aren't required to concentrate on one idea for any length of time. Don't worry if you found your mind wandering after a couple of seconds. You're just out of practice. The more you practice concentrating, either by meditation or an exercise like this one, the better you'll get at it.

Many good books on meditation, and lots of links to how-to articles, can be found online. Some teachers recommend guided meditation, while others promote a mantra or even complete internal silence. It's more important to find a technique that fits you and your lifestyle, than to do what some guru says is the "only way." Find a meditation style that you like, because if you like it, you'll do it regularly. If you're meditating regularly, you're learning to tune in to your sixth sense while tuning out distractions from the other five. Whether you meditate with the express purpose of developing your abilities, or just for general relaxation, there are many, many guided meditations you should be able to access. I've included a couple of meditations in the next chapter, to help you get started.

Impressions As Symbols

Recognizing your predominant learning channel and developing concentration skills are the foundation of mediumship. Now that you're ready to tune in to the other side, it's time to learn the language of symbols.

So much more information can be conveyed with a symbol, than with just a word. Consider the symbol for Neighborhood Watch groups: a simple graphic of a thief lifting a window. To the neighbors, this symbol conveys a sense of community, of watching out for each other, and being ready to ask questions or call the police should someone suspicious turn up. It means homeowners actively patrol the streets of their neighborhood, and everyone is expected to participate. It says, "We care about our homes, and we're going to be safe here."

This symbol represents something entirely different to the potential burglar, however. It says, "You are *not* safe to lurk around here." If all of these words and sentiments had to be written out, including the different messages to the different people, it wouldn't make for a very efficient sign.

Spirit people use symbols, too. They've shown me that they have limited time or energy to communicate with us, so getting a message across via symbols is an efficient use of their resources. By impressing a symbol on my mind, they are able to give me not only a visual description, but a description of their emotions, relationship, gender, disease, or message, all at once. They do this not by downloading some random idea into my head, but by stirring up something in my own mind, that is symbolic of their message. They literally get me to think about something from my own past experience. It's then my job to interpret this personal recollection, and relate it to my client.

In your mind, you have a whole entire library of experiences. No one else in the world has this library, just you. This collection of experiences includes emotions, actual events, sensations, input from your physical senses, memories—in essence, every single thing you've ever experienced. It's almost like a language all your own. If I want to communicate in French, for example, I know that I first need to access my own personal experience in the English language. Only then I can associate that with a word in French. Take the French verb *manger,* which means "to eat." Unless I know what "to eat" means in English, learning *manger* will be completely outside of my understanding. It would be impossible to translate or communicate.

Mediumship works the same way. As a medium, you need to translate impressions that come through clairsentience, clairvoyance, or clairaudience, into words and sentences in your own language. How can you do that? By relying on the experiences in your own library. All you have, and all the spirits have if they want to communicate with you, is your own library. If you're getting a message from a spirit who spoke only French when he was alive, and you don't speak French, you're not going to get impressions in French. It's that simple. The spirit person is going to give you his message with symbols that you understand.

Everyone's library of experiences is unique. There isn't one universal symbol for anything, because everyone has had different life experiences. For one person, an impression of a dog may bring up feelings of loyalty. For someone who is afraid of dogs, getting this impression will trigger a totally different interpretation. Everyone has had unique experiences, so symbols can mean completely different things to different people. That's why you can't be wrong in your interpretation, and why you shouldn't compare yourself to other mediums. The spirit people will find a way to get their message to you. Over time you'll develop a library of symbols that will be available to all the spirit people who come through to you.

Below I list some of the common symbols the spirit people have taught me. They are unique to my experience, so if you perceive something different in your own practice, go with your own impressions. You can see my symbols are a mixture of visual impressions and feelings, because I am clairvoyant and clairsentient:

- A box with a bow on it means "Happy Birthday"
- A handful of balloons means "Happy Birthday" to a child
- A bouquet of roses symbolizes an anniversary, either of a wedding or the spirit's passing
- The cancer ribbon shown sideways over one part of the body, means cancer began there and moved someplace else, or started someplace else and settled there
- A cross means the spirit was very devout, or in the ministry
- A cross on its side means my guest or her spirit person changed the practice of faith; it can also mean laying down a heavy burden
- Feeling a *zing!* up my spine means the connection has been made, or that I'm correct, and I should continue
- Seeing dark clouds in front of a spirit's eyes means she had vision

or eye trouble; it can also mean it's been a very long time since
my guest has seen her
- A spirit with his head in his hands symbolizes depression
- The image of a brain with a lightening bolt through it means
mental illness, schizophrenia, or seizures
- Feeling a sharp pop in my head symbolizes stroke or aneurism
- Feeling a sharp pain outside my skull symbolizes an impact from
without, such as a blow to the head
- When I feel that I'm struggling to breathe, I know that a spirit
person wants to tell me she suffered from lung disease or had
assistance breathing before passing
- When I have to repeatedly clear my throat, I know I'm talking
with a spirit person who was a smoker
- I have accurately represented the spirit and his message when all
feelings, images, and symptoms disappear

During a reading, a spirit gives me a combination of these generic
symbols and a series of impressions unique to herself. The real work
involves translating those unique symbols and impressions as rapidly as
they come in. This part of mediumship is like spontaneous translating,
and where confidence can waiver if you're not careful. Quite frequently,
I'll receive a quick series of symbols that will take me a minute to parse
into a coherent sentence, before translating. If I've misinterpreted the
symbols when I begin the translation, the spirit will interrupt and
correct me.

Don't second-guess yourself. When you see, hear, or feel an
impression, go with your first instinct. Don't be afraid to be wrong.
There have been many times during a reading where I'll give an
interpretation of an impression I get, only to update it, refine it, or
re-explain it altogether moments later.

If an impression or symbol makes no sense to you, don't worry.
Remember that it's not your job to understand the message, simply
to deliver it. If an impression really baffles you, ask in the quiet of
your mind for the spirit person to give you more information. If I'm
quiet for more than a minute, I'll let my client know that I'm busy
interpreting something from the spirit.

Also, take your time. If a symbol or impression is confusing, wait a moment or two. Notice if you have an emotional response to it, or if it triggers something in your memory. I once got the image of my own grandmother in spirit during a reading for a client. I had no idea what she was doing there, so I waited. The next moment I inexplicably remembered a phrase we had about my grandmother: "An iron fist in a velvet glove." *Zing!* I shared that phrase with my client, and she knew exactly who I was bringing through. A great aunt in spirit wanted to define her personality when alive. Instead of laboriously spelling it out, word by word, the spirit aunt located a memory I had. My grandmother symbolized "an iron fist in a velvet glove," so the spirit person prompted me to remember her.

Above all, remember that in addition to the pictures, sounds, or feelings you get, most of what you'll be receiving will be symbols. Assume that they are for you to interpret, using whatever memories they trigger, or feelings they bring up. If you're unsure whether the impression is symbolic or literal, just wait. An impression that is meant to be symbolic will be followed by a memory or an emotion. That's your cue to start talking. An impression that is literal will not be followed by anything, but will simply linger. That's your cue to share exactly what you're getting. Like the octopus I mentioned in the Introduction, the impression may persist until you interpret it correctly.

CHAPTER 20

Exercises and Guided Meditations

I use the following guided meditations in many of my psychic development classes. I recommend reading them into a recorder, and playing them back when you want to practice. You can also loosely memorize them.

Don't be discouraged if meditation feels difficult at first. Focus and concentration take practice, so don't be too hard on yourself. This is supposed to be fun!

Also, feel free to adapt the script to your preferences. When I began, I used to imagine I was diving into a deep, cool, pool of water, where my five senses were muffled. I would imagine that the spirit people would swim up to me. That was how my logical mind could make sense of the indistinct visuals that define clairvoyance. Now I sometimes meditate for awareness in my cells and thoughts, so I can develop greater knowledge of energy, and so that I can use my clairvoyant eyes as I do my hands.

There's no right or wrong way to meditate, so keep trying till you find a style you enjoy, and practice, practice, practice! Let your intuition guide you when it comes to trying different styles. I may use one type of meditation technique for several weeks or months, and then move on to something new. I constantly reinterpret how I want to move forward in developing my own abilities, so I adapt my approach to spirit communication techniques all the time. Keeping a journal may be a helpful way to track your progress. Just be sure to remain flexible as your abilities expand. What works when you're beginning may not fit as your skills evolve.

Both this meditation and the following one are available as pre-recorded audio files on my website, **www.liveandlearnguides.com**.

Guided Meditation for Spirit Communication

Get comfortable, close down your eyes, and begin to pay attention to your breathing. You don't have to do anything special with your breath—just notice it. Notice your breathing, in and out. Observing your breathing in and out, notice how it becomes a little more relaxed, perhaps a little shallower. Tell yourself now that every breath out will continue to relax you. It's safe to relax, healthy for both the body and the mind. Every easy breath in refreshes you, and every easy breath out relaxes you, more and more, as all distraction drains away.

In a moment you're going to imagine something—just play along, pretend if you have to. Using your imagination and concentrating are the two most important things you can do to get in tune with and develop your own extra-sensory perception.

Imagine that there is a light in the middle of your chest, right where your heart is. Imagine that every time you inhale you're adding energy to that light—like an old-fashioned bellows blowing gently on embers, oxygen feeds the fire making it glow brighter and grow stronger. Every time you breathe in, this light gets a little brighter and bigger. And every time your heart beats, it sends some of this light out in to your body, along with healthy, oxygen-rich blood. It takes just three minutes for blood to be sent from your heart out to the very tips of your blood vessels and back again. Now your heart beats are sending light energy too, all the way down to the tips of your fingers and toes, and in three minutes, even less now, your whole entire body will be filled with this perfect glowing light. As you listen, this light continues to circulate through your body, bringing light, healing, and total relaxation.

Picture again the light in the middle of your chest. Think about a bead of this light separating and traveling up your spine, through your neck, through your jaw, behind your cheeks and eyes, and coming gently to rest, right behind the middle of your forehead.

Bring your attention to this light, watch it, feel it, or just imagine it pulsing quietly and gently there, stimulating your second sight.

As you concentrate on this light, all outside distractions begin to fall away. There may be sounds around you, but let them diminish in importance. You may be aware of feelings in your physical body, but let them seem far away and unimportant. This gentle, persistent light focuses your energy, imagination and thoughts on a deep and subtle level.

Continue to keep your eyes, your thoughts or your feelings focused on this light behind your forehead. Concentrate on it. If your thoughts stray, just bring them back. Concentration takes practice, so don't be too concerned if you find it difficult in the beginning—just keep returning your attention to this light.

Now, gently, softly, without breaking your concentration, let the spirit people know that this light means you're ready to communicate with them. Invite a loving spirit person to come forward. And then....wait...

(Turn off the recorder here for as long as you like).

What first came to mind? What just seemed to pop into your head? Did you see an impression of a person? Did it seem like you heard someone? Or did you get a feeling? Does it seem as though you're in the presence of a man or a woman. How do you know?

Let more information come through from the spirit person. Ask questions if you want to. Record your thoughts by gently taking notes or by speaking into a recorder. You may also choose to simply remember what you're experiencing.

Thank that spirit person for the efforts and invite in another one, or prepare to close your communication. Take as much time as you like.

When you're ready to end your meditation, imagine the light begins to dim. This signals to the spirit people that you stopping for now. As the light fades, allow yourself to come gently to full awareness.

Guided Meditation to Connect With Spirit Guides

Get comfortable, close down your eyes, and begin to pay attention to your breathing. You don't have to do anything special with your breath, just breathe in and out as you normally do. Just by paying attention to your breathing, you naturally become aware of HOW you're breathing, so simply observe that. Imagine when you breathe in how your lungs gather the oxygen from that breath and move it right into your blood stream. Every cell in your body is taking part in every breath you take in and breathe out. Tell yourself now that every breath out will relax you more and more. It's safe to relax, healthy for both the body and the mind. Every easy breath in refreshes you, and every easy breath out relaxes you, more and more, as all distraction drains away.

Imagine you're stepping into an elevator. If for some reason you are uncomfortable in elevators, pretend that this one is as large as a room, very comfortable and safe. Imagine yourself stepping into this private, comfortable, safe elevator and locating the panel near the door. On this panel are buttons numbered from 1 to 10. As you step into this elevator and think about this panel, you notice that the number 1 is lit up from behind. Reach now, in your mind's eye, and push the number 10 button. See or imagine it lighting up now.

However you want this elevator to be, think about it now. Look around it or create it in your mind. Some people like glass elevators, where they can see the landscape spread out around them as they rise. Others prefer a luxuriously appointed cozy space, with comfy lounge chairs and beautiful music playing softly in the background. If you're one of the people who likes to have an elevator operator opening and closing the doors and operating the levers to get you to your floor, imagine him or her now, quietly following your request to go to the 10th floor.

Get comfortable for this ride. Sit down. Stretch out. This is going to be very, very relaxing.

Think about the elevator starting to rise now. As it moves from Level 1 to Level 2, tell yourself that you're temporarily leaving behind all of your cares and worries, your entire To Do list, mental projects and physical discomforts—all being left on the first level. Imagine your expectations being left there, too. Don't worry; when you return to this level you can pick them up again, or even leave them for the staff to gather up and discard. All of your stuff will be safe there.

As you approach the second level, you are dropping away—just for now—all distractions and disruptions, allowing you to focus and concentrate on the very special journey you're on.

See the 2 button light up on the panel as you pass this floor. Still rising at a very comfortable and safe pace, you begin to feel a deep relaxation spread through your body—almost like you're leaving the force of gravity behind as you rise. Your body feels increasingly calm and relaxed, maybe even weightless or numb. Shoulders, neck, jaw... all relaxing more and more. Back, belly, chest... so comfortable. All of your organs functioning perfectly in a state of relaxation and good health. Your hips, legs and feet relax and let go, every nerve, muscle, tendon, bone and cell... just relax and let go.

Now as you approach the third level, you may even experience yourself kind of spreading out, softening around the edges. Maybe you begin to feel like your edges are expanding or blurring a bit. The way an ice cube melts and spreads out, think about your wonderful energy, your wonderful self, naturally and easily just taking up a little more space. See the 3 button on the panel light up, and imagine yourself expanding.

Every breath out continues to relax you, and bring you gently and safely out of conscious association with the body, and into conscious connection with your higher mind.

See the 4 button light up on the panel now. Imagine you are high above the earth, so if you were to peak out you'd see half the world below you, the curve of the far edge of the earth. Twinkling lights from the cities, lines of car lights moving like blood pulsing through veins. Very safe, very comfortable, very, very calm. You are open to whatever this experience brings you; you have left your expectations behind, and you give yourself permission to accept whatever comes to you.

Imagine now that the 5 button on the panel illuminates. You're half way there. You never felt safer or more imaginative or more relaxed than you feel now. Your energy is taking up it's natural place in the world—an ever-expanding self that is connected to everything above and below. Like a vapor or a soft cloud, growing and moving, uncontained and uncontainable. You may even have a sense that you can look down at yourself now, resting here. You know on all the levels of your mind that you are completely and totally safe, and that your body is reverting to the healthiest it's ever been.

The 6 button lights up. Still rising, imagine you feel a growing weightlessness, or dissociation from your body. Imagine you can look out and see the earth far below you, and if you focus you can see a strong, unbreakable cord from you—where you are now in your mind—to your body and your home far below. Breathing naturally and normally, every breath out relaxes you more and more, expanding your ability to imagine and to trust that imagination.

Seven. Allow yourself to feel a growing anticipation, butterflies or a kind of excitement, as you are about to reunite with best friends, loved ones, teachers and healers. What an exciting and happy reunion that will be. You will recognize your guides and you will be recognized by them. What a joyful, hearty greeting you can expect. At this reunion you'll remember the guides you meet again, and hear their good counsel, and take comfort in their presence. Breathe, relax, look forward.

The 8 button lights up now as you feel the elevator begin to slow down. Look outside: all around you there are stars. You're deep in a star forest: stars above you and below you, on either side, beautiful, perfect, silent stars. Tranquility, serenity, peace. You are here: perfect, whole, complete, and beloved. One with this living, breathing universe: part of it and all of it at the same time. Imagine you can feel the timelessness of this place. Breathing in perfection, you breathe out disbelief.

Somewhere, in the back of your mind, you become aware of passing the ninth level, still rising, expanding, reconnecting and recovering your birthright of total joy, peace and love. What a happy moment! A moment that continues on and on for all eternity. You belong here.

Now, 10. The elevator has dropped away, but waits for you where you can find it when it's time to return.

Take a moment to settle your awareness. You might want to look—with your eyes closed—at a point somewhere between your eyebrows, or at some other imagined place. Keep your focus here.

Now, very gently, check in with the energy on your right side. Imagine you can feel a presence there, or approaching you there. Don't question yourself, just allow yourself to feel as though someone very respectful comes towards you. Answering with the first thing that comes to mind, ask yourself—does this someone feel male or female? Trust your first instinct, just go with it for now.

Some people have a visual impression, some seem to hear the information, still others feel it come in the same way an idea pops into your head. Let it be how it is for you. The more you concentrate, the more often you come here or the longer you stay, the more quickly and easily you will trust your own senses and the information that comes through. Let yourself once again check in with the energy on your right side. Male? or Female? Whatever seems to be the loudest, or brightest, or whatever seems to stick— just go with it.

Stay focused with your eyes closed and your mind open, just as you are now. Let more information come through from the being on your right. In what capacity does this being guide you? For the moment, as support for this specific time in your life, or does he or she intend to stay with you through your lifetime? Does this guide work specifically with you on something, such as love, creativity, health or life purpose? Ask these questions or any others that come to mind, and note what answers first seem to come to you.

Very often our guides don't use words, but convey their thoughts to us—which means guidance from them can feel like we're just thinking our own thoughts or making up our own answers. Let the analysis go for now, just receive what your mind is making you aware of, and don't worry too much about the mechanics of how those thoughts got there.

You may want to ask if the guide on your right goes by a certain name. You'll know you have an answer when a name or other sound just occurs to you. It may be something silly or something a little too human to seem real to you right now—but just remember, our guides want to make us comfortable, so they're going to present themselves in a way that is believable and acceptable. Many don't want to be called anything in particular and will allow you to call them whatever you like. Some people just get an initial. Listen or become aware of your response to that question, and accept it just for now.

Still focused on that point you're looking at with closed eyes, take a moment to feel or think about who may be on your left. Feel or imagine energy that is waiting there or that is approaching you. Is this energy male or female? Large or small? Constantly there or taking a turn as your guide for a certain reason. By what name may you call this energy on the left?

Now, look around you or think about looking around you with your mind's eye: is there anyone else there? Another spirit guide, or perhaps even someone you know who has crossed over? You may find you're enjoying a quiet meeting with your guide or guides, or you may find yourself in the middle of a big party of spirit people who have all come to greet you and reconnect with you.

Take a few moments to become familiar with the way you're feeling, with the energy of your guides, and with how information comes in.

Maybe you have a specific question you'd like to ask your guides. Ask it now, and listen for the answer. You'll remember everything you're experiencing. Your guides may answer you with direct information, or may suggest a way for you to discover the answer yourself. If you find that no answer is coming, ask your guides if they want you to know the answer now—perhaps part of your life plan is to discover the answer to this challenge on your own.

Now, turn your attention to the guide on your right, and ask for a sign from this guide that you are being answered. When you want to ask this guide for help, or when this guide wants to get your attention, let there be a signal of some sort that you can be aware of in your regular, waking state. Maybe it's an image of something, or maybe a feeling in your body. Maybe you'll hear a buzzing or ringing in your ears.

Ask the guide on your right for something now. Trust what you get, even if it feels slight. If you are feeling, hearing, seeing, or thinking about something, and you wonder if this is the signal, ask your guide now to confirm by making that feeling, image, sound, or thought brighter, louder, or stronger.

Now turn your attention to the energy on your left side, and ask for a signal from this guide. It's likely to be different, so be open to a new impression. Take your time, double-check by asking again or by asking the guide to intensify the sign.

All of your guides are here to support you. They are your support team on the other side. Before you came in you worked with them to set up challenges, to learn lessons, to overcome fears. They are here at your disposal during those difficult times, and want so much to help you, to remind you that everything is going to be all right. They know, and your higher mind knows, that everything will turn out okay, so you can be free of fear or worry or distress.

Feel free to stay a while longer with your guides and loved ones in spirit. When you're done, you'll be able to gently return to your five physical senses easily and quickly. If you intend to return to your waking state now, imagine stepping back into that elevator. Call it and have it appear before you, and settle yourself within it now. You can always return to this level whenever you want to. Reach in your mind's eye and push the number 1 button on the panel. Imagine the elevator begins to descend as you count yourself down from 10 to 1. When you reach the number 1, you'll open your eyes feeling wide awake and alert, and more confident than ever before in your ability to communicate with your spirit guides.

Automatic Writing

When a person writes without conscious awareness of what they're putting on paper, we call it automatic writing. The words are said to come from the subconscious mind or from a spirit source, and not from the writer's own thoughts or ideas. This can happen in a trance or waking state. Inspired writing is very similar, but the writer has the conscious awareness of what she's writing, as it's being written. Automatic writing is not particular to mediumship. As a clinical hypnotist, I've used automatic writing to help my clients locate lost objects or recall something buried deeply in the mind.

Although many automatic writing instruction guides recommend using pen and paper, I've had much more success with a keyboard. It's easier for me to type quickly, than to write longhand. Choose whichever method is easiest or most relaxing for you, regardless of what the instruction guides say. If you practice with the honest intention to seek answers or information, the tool—whether pen or keyboard—won't interfere with the message. Also, don't get too caught up in where the information is coming from. We have access to the wisdom deep in our own minds, as well as that which comes from the spirit world. Both sources are valuable. When I practice automatic writing, I can't be absolutely certain that the words coming through are from my own subconscious mind's higher understanding, or from the spirit people. In the end, it doesn't matter. When you read what you've written, either for yourself or a client, you'll know whether it feels true and valid.

You may or may not find yourself in a deep trance when you're practicing. Don't get too caught up in that either. Relaxing into the exercise is the key. You'll know you're in the right frame of mind when ideas and words flow easily. Try not to read what you're writing as you practice; your conscious mind will want to jump in and make corrections. Save the editing until your session is done. And don't worry if what you're writing doesn't make sense right away. Just practice getting into the flow of translating impressions onto paper.

If you feel like writing will engage too much of your rational mind, or will jar you out of the trance state, try speaking into a recorder. I used to do that all the time in the beginning. Now I prefer to type when I practice automatic writing, because I can type without looking at the keyboard. This allows me to type with my eyes closed, which is very helpful for a clairvoyant person.

Feel free to practice with other media, too. If you're a painter or like to sketch, use the process outlined below before picking up a brush or charcoal. If you're a musician, do the exercise before sitting down with your instrument. Even dancers and choreographers can use this method. Just substitute the writing terms with terms that apply to your medium.

Guided Automatic Writing Exercise

Get into a comfortable position, in front of your keyboard or with pen and paper nearby.

If you like, type or write a particular question at the top of the page, or simply pose it in your mind before beginning. This is optional, but a great way to set your intention and develop trust in the process.

Close your eyes and pay attention to your breathing. Inhale through your nose to a count of 5, hold the breath for a few seconds, and exhale through your mouth to a count of 5. Do this several times. The number itself isn't important; this just helps you to concentrate on your breathing.

Tell yourself that when your higher mind is ready to bring information either through its own wisdom or from a spirit person, that your hands will naturally and automatically reach for the keyboard or the pen. Suggesting this to yourself gives your subconscious mind permission to begin when ready.

Begin to relax your body with any method you're familiar or comfortable with. You can relax by focusing on each body part from the head down or the toes up. You can imagine yourself going down a set of stairs, relaxing with each step you take. You can even imagine drifting down a lazy river, relaxing every time you exhale.

Deepen your trance, by counting from 10 down to 1. Tell yourself that with each number, your conscious mind will relax, while your subconscious mind rises to the surface. Repeat the suggestion that when you're ready, your hands will automatically and effortlessly reach for the keyboard or pen.

When you feel even the slightest urge to do so, pick up your pen and pad, or rest your fingers on the keyboard. If you're holding a pen, begin doodling loosely. If you're using a keyboard, just begin tapping out a random rhythm with your fingers. The purpose is to begin to move muscles while staying in the trance state.

If you find your trance lightening, keep your pen or fingers moving randomly, while counting from 5 down to 1. Tell yourself once again that with each number, your conscious mind relaxes and slides out of the way.

When you feel sentences or thoughts coming together, trust that your hand or fingers will translate them to the paper. Don't worry if you're writing complete sentences. Be light and playful. I sometimes will actively engage my mind so that I won't double-check what I'm writing. I do that by humming a song in my mind or picturing my dog's goofy smile while my fingers are moving.

Go for as long as it takes. When you're done, you'll know it. If it's thirty seconds or thirty minutes, it doesn't matter. Read what you've written or set it aside for an hour or so, and then go back.

Keep practicing! Even if your first couple of sessions don't reveal anything profound, keep at it. Trust the process, refrain from self-judgment, and have confidence.

I have a friend who kept a journal of all the automatic writing she did. She would take a few minutes to practice, three or four times a week, and she never looked back to read what she'd written. After several months she re-read her entries, and was astonished to discover that she had accurately predicted major events in the national news, and in her local community. She'd even predicted major incidents in her family life. What a valuable tool she created for herself! With her automatic writing, she feels much more prepared to handle all of life's challenges.

The Psychic Grid

Years ago I created something I call a psychic grid. I've never shared it with anyone, even with my students, before now. It helped tremendously when I was getting started, and I still consult it regularly. Obviously, this is a subjective device, and with consistent use you'll adapt it to your own degrees of measurement.

It all began when I noticed that some mediumship sessions were truly fantastic, and others simply good. I couldn't see it yet, but I suspected that certain factors were influencing the spirit connections. I was always able to bring spirit people in, and my clients all left satisfied, but some sessions were obviously better than others. I started by grading each reading or circle after it was done, using the typical academic grading system: A, B, C, D, and F. The grade was for the overall level of energy, spirit connection, guest involvement, and my facility in translating for the spirit people. For example, an "A" grade reflected a high level of excitement and emotion, lots of laughter, multiple spirit connections with fine detail, and clearly meaningful messages. Connections in an "A" session are rapid-fire and highly significant, and guests and room are buzzing.

Over time I factored in other elements I could think of that might impact a session, from my mood to the weather. After several months I plotted my results on a chart, and discovered strong associations between "A" readings and certain factors in my inner and outer environment. I will admit that I became a little obsessive about my grid, until I determined that relying too much on environmental factors could, in fact, limit me.

Below is a copy of my grid, adapted over the years. Feel free to add in your own elements or remove some of those listed here. Customize it to reflect tools you use, such as tarot cards, scrying mirrors, or runes.

A word of warning: the mind can be highly suggestible. Let your grid be a way of keeping records, rather than determining how you must always go forward or succeed. If your grid shows that you have fantastic results when it's stormy outside, don't let that trigger a mindset of defeat if you have an appointment scheduled on a beautiful sunny day. If the environmental factors aren't present for a reading, meditate on them to bring their energy in.

GUESTS	
Days between scheduling & circle	
Which guest made appointment?	
Any repeat clients in group?	
Number of people present	
Men:Women	
Family members present	
Average # of spirit people/person	
Any clients resistant/testing?	
Client chimney?	
Guest Name:	Best Connection:
Guest Name:	Best Connection:
Guest Name:	Best Connection:
Guest Name:	Best Connection:

ENVIRONMENT	
Location of circle	
Date	
Time	
Chimney in location?	
Weather	
Barometric pressure	
Temperature	
Moon phase	
Season	
PERSONAL (all ratings 1-10, lowest-highest)	
Most recent meal	
Any alcohol within 24 hours?	
Any exercise today?	
Mood (1-10)	
Colors & fabric I'm wearing	
Metal or stone jewelry I'm wearing	
What day of monthly cycle?	
Sleep well last night?(1-10)	
Stress level before circle (1-10)	
Meditation today? Value (1-10)	
Meditate before circle?	
Which meditation?	
Personal relationships okay?	
Any other clients before circle?	
Confidence (1-10)	

HIGHLIGHTS (note down stand-out connections)	
Overall Grade:	

Fill out a grid after each reading or circle. When you have gathered data from several circles, collect those with an "A" grade, and note what those circles have in common. It may be something as simple as a wearing a certain color, or foregoing a glass of wine the night before. There's no evidence that the factors that contribute to an "A" circle actually affect the spirit connection. Those factors could simply be combining to result in a positive self-regard, which affects confidence levels. If wearing blue, taking a yoga class, getting along with my sweetheart, and having slept well contribute to an elevated mood and high confidence, I'm almost certainly going to have a better reading.

The spirit people are always encouraging us to be less serious or rigid. Have fun with this grid. If using it helps you manage your abilities and clients with less stress, see it as the tool it is. If using the grid becomes more of a hindrance than a help, set it aside.

CHAPTER 21

What's Next?

If you think you're getting a message from a spirit person, or a spirit has come into your presence, it's important to **acknowledge them.** Even if I'm alone in the kitchen and I feel a loved one come up to me, I always say, "Hi Grandma!" or personally greet whoever I feel it is.

Concentrate fully on your impression of the spirit person by tuning in. Tuning in is really more like tuning out, or ignoring the environment and what registers for your physical senses. It takes concentration to ignore the obvious and focus on the subtle. Did you ever look up and see someone looking right at you? It's because on some level, you had an awareness of another person's energy in your space. That awareness usually doesn't make it to the conscious level. We don't say to ourselves, "*I feel like someone is looking at me, let me look around and see.*" Yet somewhere inside our minds we register that someone else's energy has come into our personal mind-space. Do the same thing with spirit people. When you recognize that "in my space" feeling, instead of looking up, just stay focused on the energy that has come into your mind. Become deaf and blind to your environment. If you wait, and concentrate on that other energy, more information will follow. It will be subtle of course, but allow it in anyway. Don't worry if it makes sense or not. If appropriate, talk aloud about the information you see, hear or feel.

Tuning in can involve some work. Besides concentrating, you might find that sometimes you switch from straining to see, to straining to hear, to focusing on your body to feel. Like an old-fashioned radio warming up, for me it takes time to get into the groove of a reading or message circle. Each time I tune in, I have to fiddle with the knob a bit so I get the clearest reception I can. As the radio warms up, and the spirit people and I find the best frequency to communicate, the messages come faster and more clearly. So give yourself time to warm up. That's why meditation helps right before.

If you're having trouble understanding the spirit person, ask for clarification, and wait. The most important thing you can do if you're not getting an answer or not understanding a message, is to wait. I often have entire conversations with the spirit people in my head before saying the message out loud, in my efforts to get it right.

You can also tell the spirits how you want them to impress you, especially with some of the basic information like gender, relationship to the living person, and so on. For me, when a spirit comes through from the mother's side of the family, they give me the feeling of being on my right. A paternal ancestor will be on my left. I remember specifically requesting this system so that I could more confidently communicate details to my clients.

If there is a particular spirit person you'd like to be in regular contact with, **set up a plan to communicate and practice.** If both of you are determined, the communication will happen. You may need to practice for quite a while at first, but keep up your end of the agreement, and in time your spirit person will come through clearly.

See if you can find a place to practice. I always encourage my guests to pay attention to their own intuition, and to volunteer any impressions they are receiving during my message circles. I believe everyone has the ability to receive psychic impressions or messages from spirits, and circles are a great, safe place to develop the confidence to voice what you're receiving. There may be ongoing séances in your area that you can join, or you may want to start your own with a few like-minded friends. If you're starting something new, be sure to treat your efforts with respect. It's a commitment that your guides and spirit people are entering into also.

Start giving readings whenever you can. It's easier to do with strangers, as you won't know who their spirit people are, but try it even with friends. Just ask the spirit person to give you something that you don't know, but your friend will still be able to validate. And when you get an impression—share it! You won't be able to develop confidence if you don't start getting some validation. Don't be afraid to be wrong, just say what you're receiving. I promise you, you'll amaze yourself!

Above all, *have fun.* As Sister Alma reported from the spirit world, God and the spirit people are playful, and always seem so delighted to connect with those of us still here in the physical world.

One Final Note

I remember a writer's convention I attended many years ago. It was a weekend-long event at Cornell University, that featured many workshops led by famous novelists, non-fiction authors, screen-writers, and other literary professionals. Hundreds of students like myself turned up with fresh notebooks and open minds, eager for the little-known secrets that would bring us success.

At the beginning of his workshop, one well-known author stood up in front of all of us and said, "Who here wants to be a writer?" Every hand in the room shot up, of course. That's why we were here! The author looked out at us and said, "Then go home and write."

Stunned silence filled the room as he walked away from the podium, but that simple, clear instruction resonated profoundly with me. It served me well when I made my decision to stop focusing on learning about being a psychic medium, and to start practicing my abilities. You can read about spirit communication all you want, and never get closer to the experience. Make the decision to do it, and find a way—any way—to practice. Let further study enhance what you're doing, rather than replace the doing. Don't make the mistake of thinking you have to study for a certain amount of time before you can communicate with spirit people.

You can do it right now.

RESOURCES

The following examples are a small cross-section of the many resources available to those interested in spirit communication. An online search and the New Age section of any bookstore will offer many more. Have fun exploring!

Books

On Death and Dying
Elisabeth Kübler-Ross

The Shack
William P. Young

A Course In Miracles

The Master Key System
Charles F. Haanel

Journey of Souls and *Life Between Lives*
Dr. Michael Newton

Letters from the Afterlife
Elsa Barker

Everyone's Guide to the Hereafter
Ken Akehurst

Notable Mediums

Biographies of these and other mediums may be interesting to study

Living Mediums	Deceased Mediums
John Edward	Helena Petrovna Blavatsky
James Van Praagh	Emma Hardinge Britten
Rosemary Altea	Edgar Cayce
Marisa Anderson	Jean Dixon
Sylvia Browne	Clifford Bias
Esther Hicks	Arthur Ford

Schools of Mediumship and Psychic Development

The Arthur Findlay College
www.arthurfindlaycollege.org

Holistic Studies Institute
www.holisticstudies.org

Edgar Cayce's Association for Research & Enlightenment
www.edgarcayce.org

Spiritualist Communities

Lily Dale Assembly
www.lilydaleassembly.com

Cassadaga Spiritualist Camp
www.cassadaga.org

The National Spiritualist Association of Churches
www.nsac.org

ABOUT THE AUTHOR

Priscilla Keresey is recognized throughout the country as one of the most accurate, compassionate, and sought-after psychic mediums. In addition to bringing the physical and spiritual worlds together for individuals and groups, Priscilla coordinates local psychic fairs, appears on radio and television programs, and acts as guest minister and medium for local Spiritualist churches. She is a keynote speaker at conferences on the topics of Creating Success & Prosperity, Reclaiming Your Connection to the Divine, and Using The Power of Your Inner Mind. She teaches workshops on developing psychic ability and offers training for mediums in her message circles.

Priscilla is also certified by the National Guild of Hypnotists as an Advanced Clinical Hypnotist, specializing in Past Life Regression, and she is an ordained Minister of Peace. She has created and taught a highly-effective six-week program on empowerment for female inmates in the New York State Correctional System.

Priscilla is the author of the Live & Learn Guides™, and the author and producer of the Live & Learn Guides™ self-hypnosis audio files. She resides in New York.

To contact Priscilla, use one of the following methods:

Online	Address
www.apracticalpsychic.com	P.O. Box 226
www.liveandlearnguides.com	Putnam Valley, NY 10579
www.viahypnosis.com	
	Telephone
Facebook.com/APracticalPsychic	(914) 672-9741

OTHER PRODUCTS BY PRISCILLA KERESEY

The Live & Learn Guides™ Series

Mapping Your Destiny: How to Use the Amazing Power of Intention

Do you ever wonder why some people seem to have it all? Are you having trouble getting some traction on your dreams? The quickest, most efficient way to define and create the life you want is by setting intentions. In this book you'll learn:
• How to ask for what you want (set an intention)
• What not to do when you set goals or intentions
• The no-fail formula for designing the life you've always dreamed of

Getting the Money You Want, Not Just the Money You Need: The Straight Path to Abundance

Have you read countless books on creating prosperity? Have you been to the seminars and done the visualizations and still find yourself struggling? Are you ready, now, to live in the relaxation and serenity that comes with knowing your financial needs are always taken care of? Then this is the last book you'll ever have to read! In this book you'll learn:
• What's been holding you back
• How to release it, once and for all
• The six steps to ongoing prosperity

Unveiling Your Psychic Powers: Never-Before-Told Secrets of a Psychic Medium

You may not know this, but you're already psychic. Everyone is! While it's true that some individuals seem to have an effortless "gift" of seeing the future, reading the past, or communicating with spirits, every single one of us has the same tools and abilities. We just need to learn how to use them, practice, and develop confidence. In this book you'll learn how to:
• Distinguish a psychic impression from a self-generated thought
• Read other people and situations instantly and confidently
• Build confidence in your own intuitive abilities with fun, easy exercises

A Radically Successful You: Easy New Ways to Achieve Any Goal, Fast!
Are you tired of watching your co-workers get promoted while you slog
away day after day? Do you ever wonder how your friend manages to be
in the right place at the right time, all the time? Do you compare yourself
to self-starters or entrepreneurs and wonder what they have that you
don't? You are about to learn the secrets of real success! You'll be one of
the winners – guaranteed! In this book you'll learn:
• Why you may not be succeeding right now
• How successful people deal with obstacles
• Six steps to creating and programming automatic success habits

Your Total Health Solution: 3 Ways. 7 Days. Guaranteed!
Do you have trouble turning off the chatter and relaxing, either at your
lunch break during the day or before bedtime at night? Does it feel like
it's been years since you had energy to try something new or go after
a long-held goal? Are you tired of feeling so rundown? If so, this book
offers you ways to return to total health in a shorter time than you might
have thought possible. In this book you'll learn:
• How to approach total health on three fronts simultaneously
• What steps to take for physical health now, that are easy to assimilate
• What emotional health is, and how to begin experiencing it
• What mental balance is, and how you can find it
• What to do on Day 8 and beyond.

Praying: Creating A Relationship With God
Did you ever wonder if prayer really works? Have you ever been
concerned that you're not doing it "right?" Are you repeating by rote
those old prayers from your childhood, wondering if it's really possible
that God hears that droning? You're not alone. In this book you'll learn:
• What makes a prayer a prayer
• How to create a prayer, and how to pray
• How to know your prayers are being heard and answered
• The benefits of praying
• Whether traditional prayers or "home-made" prayers are right for you.

Live & Learn Guides™ are available in printed or electronic format.
Ordering information can be found by clicking the "Products" link at
www.liveandlearnguides.com

The Live & Learn Guides™ Self-Hypnosis Audio Series

Change Your Mind, Change Your Fortune
Abundance begins in the mind. Creating a mindset that says "Yes!" to prosperity is the key first step in creating a fortune. Listen to this self-hypnosis audio file and prepare your mind to naturally, intuitively, and rapidly attract riches into your life.

Creating True Success
We get what we focus on, and when we focus on success we create more. Listening to this self-hypnosis audio file allows you to realize the many ways you're already succeeding, opening the door for increased opportunities to achieve your goals.

Lose Weight, Feel Great!
Everyone knows that a healthy weight is more than calories in and calories out. With this audio file you can re-program your inner mind and direct your body to the shape and weight you desire.

Relax & Rejuvenate
Relax, de-stress, and create total health in your body and mind. Listen, relax, and rejuvenate!

Meeting Your Spirit Guides
Take a serene and confident guided journey to the realm of the Higher Mind, where you'll connect with your spirit guides. This guided meditation is 100% successful in bringing you together with your team on the other side. Don't miss this opportunity to learn how your guides communicate with you!

Discovering Your Personal ESP
Everyone has the ability to tap into their sixth sense. With this guided meditation you'll discover what your ESP feels like, and you'll be able to practice several techniques to hone your inherent abilities and develop confidence.

Live & Learn Guides™ are available in CD or MP3 format. Ordering information can be found by clicking the "Products" link at
www.liveandlearnguides.com

NOTES